CW00738405

George Fox
A Christian Mystic

"He had the tongue of the learned,
and could speak a word in due season
to the conditions and capacities of most,
especially to them that were weary
and wanted soul's rest—being deep
in the divine mysteries
of the Kingdom of God."

*Testimony by his step-sons and step-daughters,
probably in 1691. (Page x of the first edition
of the Journal of George Fox.)*

www.gospelofthomas.info

George Fox
A Christian Mystic

Texts that reveal his personality

Selected, edited, and introduced by
Hugh McGregor Ross

evertype
2008

Published by Evertype, Cnoc Sceichín, Leac an Anfa, Cathair na Mart, Co. Mhaigh Eo, Éire. *www.evertype.com*.

Quotations from Fox first published in 1991 as *George Fox speaks for Himself* by William Sessions Ltd., York, England.

A catalogue record for this book is available from the British Library.

ISBN-10 1-904808-17-4
ISBN-13 978-1-904808-17-6

Typesetting by Michael Everson. Set in Caslon.

Cover design by Michael Everson. The painting of George Fox attributed to Sir Peter Lely (1618–1680) is courtesy of the Friends Historical Library of Swarthmore College, Swarthmore, Pennsylvania. (It is known that there is a possibility that the painting is not of Fox, nor by Lely, nor even necessarily from the period of Fox's life; nevertheless it has been iconic of Fox for more than a century.) The background on the cover, in Fox's handwriting, is taken from an epistle to the King and Parliament, 1661, courtesy of the Haverford College Library, Haverford, Pennsylvania (Quaker Collection, George Fox Papers, Coll. no. 862, box 1).

Printed and bound by LightningSource.

Contents

"Dear George"

*As he was always addressed
by those who knew him well*

Preface

It may be said of me that I am a step-son of George Fox in the eighth generation. This is through my mother Isabel née Abraham, descended from Rachel, the youngest daughter of Margaret Fell—Fox married Margaret as her second husband well on in years. In my late teens I had the good fortune that my family lived in our ancestral home Swarthmoor Hall in the north-west of England for five years. During this time my mother was writing her definitive biography of Margaret[1] and in addition all members of my family shared in escorting around the Hall the many hundreds of visitors each year, helping to bring alive the story of the early years of the Society of Friends.

The sort of thing that would happen is that at breakfast my mother would announce that she was off to one of the seventeenth century Quaker meeting houses of the area to search for early records. At dinner she would tell of what she had found—she could identify most of the authors of documents merely by their handwriting—

1 Ross, Isabel. 1949. *Margaret Fell, Mother of Quakerism*. London: Longmans, Green & Co. Second edition 1984, York: William Sessions Ltd, ISBN 0900657839.

and explain how it was told that Fox came on some track over the hills to present his message there. A few weeks later the whole family would walk that track, bringing Fox and his companions alive.

Here then were experiences, gained at a very formative stage of life, of re-creating in a particularly vivid way the life of Fox and the Fells within a family home. I am the last remaining member of my family to have had those experiences; my cousin Margaret Fell James née Abraham is the last of her family who next lived there. There can be no others, for Swarthmoor Hall has passed into the ownership of the Society of Friends—well fitted out for all the visitors, but that is different from housing its own family.

That feeling of proximity to Fox matured until in my late fifties I attended an address by the American Quaker, Lewis Benson. He had a charismatic and inspiring quality. Benson had given much of his later years to identifying what were the cardinal elements in Fox's teaching, and in re-presenting Fox's original message. He said something in the course of his talk that made me realize that at a fundamental level I had not understood Fox. Walking along the pavement of the busy road outside Friends House in London, I resolved to find out what Fox had really said. So began a research study in the Library there that extended over five years.

The first impression I had in embarking on this study, of going amongst the great number of these documents—even those only from Fox—was bewilderment. It seemed impossible to see the trees for the density of the wood. Fortunately for me, Lewis Benson's work provided invaluable signposts and guiding lights in exploring this apparent jungle. After one or two years study it became possible to see what Fox was offering.

The consequence was that I could identify the texts of greater import, and distinguish them from those of more ephemeral purpose or of a repetitive nature. This of course involved an element of judgement, of personal decision, and it could be that another worker might choose differently. Accordingly, I copied out many manuscripts, even transcribing a few verbatim and literatim—with exact copying of spelling, etc. Furthermore I developed the knack of making précis of others in which virtually all the words were Fox's. This work began with some of the printed texts, merely because they were easier to read than the seventeenth century handwriting, but was soon turned over to the manuscripts, every one of which was studied.

At about the fourth year there I had an important experience. I suddenly saw Fox as a spiritual giant, and felt that I only came up to his knees. I consider that only something equivalent to this permits a proper perspective of Fox, while at the same time it underwrites the validity of judgements especially for making selections amongst the multitude of texts.

The most important general finding at that time of this research project was to notice that when the worthy Friends of the establishment selected Fox's texts for publication soon after his death—what we call the Journal, the Epistles, and the Doctrinals—they systematically excluded certain categories. If we read near the end of William Penn's testimony to Fox, included as part of the introduction to the Journal, we can see—especially by reading between the lines—that attitudes and viewpoints were developing amongst Friends that differed from those of Fox. He even addresses some of these in epistles from his last years. Margaret Fell was more forthright, referring to one aspect as "a poor silly gospel". These must have coloured the choice made by those Friends.

What the worthy Friends were trying to do was to assert the propriety, respectability, and soundness of the Quaker movement. They wanted sobriety and serious-ness. Therefore texts that carried an individual flavour, or were replete with personal idiosyncrasies and especially anything like imaginativeness or humour, were out. In consequence, much of the essentially human qualities of Fox were lost—so that we are left baffled by what was his charismatic influence over people, and how could it be that some of his followers were so devoted to him or could affectionately address him as "Dear George".

The gravity of this for later generations, including our own, is that assessments of Fox and his teaching have been to a very great extent based on those printed books. In historians' terms, they are based on corrupted data. It is only during the twentieth century that almost all the original texts have been brought together, primarily in the majestic Quaker Library at Friends House, London. Although Henry Cadbury did splendid work amongst them in preparing his work *George Fox's 'Book of Miracles'*—a theme to which Fox attached more importance than we would, and which the worthy

Friends thought far too risky—there seems little evidence of other systematic study amongst the original primary texts.

My work was done during my fifties. I had plenty of energy. My earning-work was sufficient to support my family and household. My interest in spirituality was growing (it often does at that period of life), and Fox made a major contribution to that. I had time enough to study Fox and also maintain close working contacts with a group of others with similar interest.

Lewis Benson's pioneering work led to the formation of the New Foundation Fellowship, a Quaker "fringe" group for the re-presentation of Fox's original gospel. My research project became an active component of that, and some of its findings were issued as typed booklets. In the fifth year, however, through a change of interest and emphasis my activity with that group went into abeyance. All the working papers were put away in the loft of my house.

However, on the occasion of the commemoration of the tercentenary of George Fox's death, it seemed to me appropriate to make a selection from the results of that research for publication as the book *George Fox Speaks for Himself.*[2]

In that, attention was concentrated on quotations that aimed to fill the primary gap in our awareness of Fox's personality and approach—-that which was filtered out. Another objective was to establish longer quotations than the snippets that were then the norm, specially

---

2   Ross, Hugh McGregor. 1991. *George Fox Speaks for Himself.* York: William Sessions Ltd, ISBN 1850720819.

those covering major aspects of Fox's teachings. Many of the quotations were from manuscripts that had never been published before. Some of the quotations are given in other books, but lost in a veritable tangle of words. The plain fact is that Fox imposes on modern readers a daunting task akin to searching for gems in the dried alluvial bed of an ancient river.

Overall, in that book the selection had been guided primarily by those texts that revealed for us Fox's distinctive qualities of personality and his innovative spiritual teachings, so that it could be said that through them George Fox speaks for himself.

Subsequently, all those working papers and the printed books accompanying them were donated to the Archive of the Brynmor Jones Library at Hull University. There they are marshalled in files, based on subject matter, and their titles can be found on their internet website.[3]

---

3   Start at **http://slb-archives.hull.ac.uk/DServe/**; click "Use this link" at the bottom of that page. Click "Search the catalogue" and enter "DRO" in the "AnyText" box. Relevant files are: DRO/11 *Notes made upon pamphlets of George Fox, including comments, precis and quotations*; DRO/15 *Notes on the epistles of George Fox, including comments, précis and quotations*; DRO/20 *Transcripts and precis of manuscript papers by George Fox bound with the 'Annual catalogue'*; DRO/17 *Notes on the structure of Fox's 'Annual catalogue'*; DRO/18 *Notes on 'a reconstruction of the manuscript pages bound up with Fox's "Annual catalogue"'*; DRO/19 *List of manuscripts included with the 'Annual catalogue'*; DRO/8 *Lists of Fox's published documents (taken from Joseph Smith's 'A descriptive catalogue of Friends books' (1867) and manuscript sources).*

Now in my nineties, and much further along the spiritual path, I realize that Fox's real achievement, the great contribution he made, was to display the qualities of a Christian mystic. He attained the ultimate mystical Experience, and it transformed his life, converting him into a charismatic spiritual giant.

In this book pride of place is given to a detailed description that he dictated at a mature age of the events and his feelings as he approached and went through that Experience.

Whereas most mystics are content to live in the glowing life that results from the Experience, Fox is distinguished by wishing to share it with others. The description he left tells the start of that, and subsequent quotations from his writings show how he went about it.

The community he founded is now known as the Religious Society of Friends, or Quakers. Relying on the structure he devised, it has survived for three and a half centuries. Admittedly there have been times when it departed from its original direction, often in response to trends in the outer community, but there have always been deeply-rooted and soundly-based Friends who have pulled it back into shape.

Introduction

A mystic is one who has had the experience
that the divine Ultimate and the essence
of the individual Self are fundamentally
one and the same.

In his mature years George Fox dictated a record of
his experiences during his eventful life. It took the
form of a Journal. It is not an autobiography in the
usual sense—-its nature may be discerned from the sub-
title it has been given: "A Historical Account of the Life,
Travels, Suffering, Christian Experience and Labour of
Love in the Work of the Ministry of George Fox". After
his death in 1681 a hand-written copy of this was passed
to Thomas Ellwood to prepare a printed version.
Ellwood had good literary ability, knew Fox personally
and greatly admired him. He wanted to do his very best
for Fox, and was guided by others who also had known
him.

During my study already referred to, it became clear
that there is some discontinuity in the account as
presented by Ellwood of a crucial experience of Fox in

his early years. However, by a simple reconstruction, merely switching two halves of the edited document, a coherent account is revealed of Fox attaining to the ultimate mystical Experience. The first quotation which follows comprises this reconstructed text.

In Fox's account he describes how, and in what ways, he lived out this Experience in his ordinary outward life. This involved many departures from the social norm and practice of his time.

One particular outcome of his Experience was a decision to share its enlivening qualities with others. To this end he began travelling and addressing crowds of people wherever he could find or gather them. This led to the establishment of the community of people now known as the Quakers. At its heart is a spiritual component. The arrangements for running this devised by Fox and his co-worker Margaret Fell have enabled the Society to survive for three and a half centuries. This is a marked contrast to the other sects which sprang up at that time, which have all since disappeared.

George Fox, and everyone else in England who met him, lived in a time when all the earlier certainties of social and personal life had been eroded, and still were being eroded. It was a period of intense flux. The feudal system, which had regulated the relationships and responsibilities of each man and woman within the social structure, had largely evaporated. Less than a century before, the iron grip of the Catholic Church had been broken by Henry VIII. Allegiance to the Catholic or Protestant Churches had become literally a matter of life and death. The Protestant Churches were springing up in many different hues, each contesting with the others. It was a time of proliferation of sects.

As a young man Fox and all his contemporaries had lived through the Civil War, and the execution of the supreme figure in the land, Charles I. This in turn was a reflection of the shift of administrative power from the ruling monarchy to a parliament of senior gentry throughout the country. During Fox's lifetime that took exaggerated form in the government led by Cromwell.

As part of the changes in the Churches, the Bible and the liturgy became available in the English language, and the development of printing made it possible for individual families to possess a copy, and soon even copies small enough to be carried about—-Fox writes "I would get into the orchards and fields with my bible, by myself." What we regard as the landmark King James version was, in his early years, a very 'new English Bible' with all the attraction of freshness.

A crucial consequence of this was a search by many people for a revised source and sense of authority, especially at the intangible level of their spiritual lives. Fox responded from his own Experience of finding an inner authority, and he shared this with others by expressing it in Biblical terms.

It is important, however, to recognize that Fox did not use the Bible in the literal way like a present-day Christian "fundamentalist". Fox used his spiritual capability to be highly selective in the passages he quoted, and he strove to discern the purport of the ancient writers and the intention of their meaning. This is a quality that makes his use and quotation of the Bible of great value to us today, even engendering a greater appreciation of that Christian book.

A feature of Fox's speech and writing that a modern reader may find difficult is his criticism of the clergy—- the "priests" he called them. Their function and role then, and their position in society, was very different from the way it is today. Because the Church was very closely linked to the government and authority of the country, it played an important part in the guidance and direction of the people. It was the law of the land that every person had to attend church services each week. These had to be held only in consecrated premises. Each household had to contribute in a material way to the Church, a system of tithes. The local clergy had a responsibility to report to the magistrates any failure in observing these laws.

At that time any member of a congregation was allowed to speak during the service after the priest had given his sermon. George Fox took advantage of this, and his ministry must often have infuriated the preacher. Because of that, and no doubt other reasons, priests roused the people to what can only be called mob-violence. Fox's Journal describes many occasions when he was severely treated. Nevertheless it was primarily the doctrinal and spiritual differences that led to Fox's criticism of the priests.

To try to omit, or edit out, this component of criticism from his quotations would amount to a severe distortion, and would detract from a significant aspect of the presentation of his personality.

We cannot expect to find any open or explicit profession of Fox's mystical Experience in any document surviving from the seventeenth century. Although in some traditions it is regarded as the goal or high point of the spiritual life, in Christianity it has always been regarded as a blasphemy, which at that time was treated with the utmost severity.[1]

Instead, we have to read between the lines of the records passed down to us, and to recognize the consequences and manifestations in Fox's life, character and teachings resulting from that Experience.

George Fox dictated over 5000 texts, as they are referred to in this book. These were taken down in shorthand or longhand, and transcribed. He wrote hardly anything himself, it is thought he had a form of dyslexia, and his own very laboured handwriting is usually found only in annotations, corrections or endorsements to the transcriptions—although we do still have his penbox with its inkwell and sand sifter for blotting.

After his great mystical Experience, the culmination of what he called his "openings", he resolved to share his illumination with others. It is described in a text from

---

1   Margaret Fell was born an Askew, it being a tradition in the family that she was a descendant of Anne Askew (it still is). At the time of Henry VIII, Anne was tortured to death, not by the usual torturer or executioner, but by two high officers of state. It was for much less than uttering a blasphemy. Of course George Fox also knew that.

his maturity—looking back on those events and decisions of his youth—that begins this book. This began his ministry which extended from 1647 to 1690, and resulted in the establishment of the Religious Society of Friends or Quakers as they were dubbed in scorn. During his ministry it may be said that he expended one third of his time and effort on sharing his illumination with others, one third in supporting and succouring his followers in the persecutions that befell them, and one third in and recovering from prison. His creation of texts each and every one with spiritual content of significance, at the phenomenal average rate of more than two each week, even continued while in prison. It meant that one or another of his followers who had the ability to record his dictation were there with him. Who do we now know of such charismatic personality as to attract such volunteers?

These texts may be classified thus: there were letters to individuals giving guidance, encouragement or support; open letters or epistles that were written for the groups of his followers—Meetings or local congregations—the establishment of which he regarded as very important; texts that were printed soon after being dictated, either as broadsheets or as pamphlets; and books, but only two of those and then jointly with other authors.

Other Publishers of Truth, as they first called themselves, also wrote epistles and pamphlets. A practice was soon established that when a manuscript epistle was received at a Meeting two Friends would be appointed, one to make a copy and the other to check for accuracy.

In this way the messages were disseminated. All the evidence indicates that texts were not distorted.

Soon after the start of Fox's mission, when the need had arisen to communicate in writing, Margaret Fell began to collect the texts of Fox and other early Quakers, and also to keep correspondence. The home of Judge Thomas Fell and Margaret, Swarthmoor Hall in a remote corner of north-west Lancashire, became the centre for the growing movement. Much information flowed to and from there, Margaret adding her own contributions such that she has been called "the nursing mother of Quakerism". In due course a great collection especially of manuscripts had been made. When in 1759 Swarthmoor Hall was sold out of the Fell family, this collection was split up amongst her many descendants. It being known that Margaret, no doubt with Fox's approval, had made this collection as a service for future generations, through all the intervening years the members of the family respected and guarded what had been received. During the twentieth century, it however became more realistic to pass these old documents to the Library of Friends House in London. It is thought that almost all the original collection is now there (with copies of a few in America).

In addition, during the seventeenth and eighteenth centuries other Quakers made systematic collections of the printed broad-sheets and pamphlets, and in some cases listed or catalogued them. These also have now come to the Library at Friends House. An exceptionally valuable item is a great handwritten folio book known as the Annual Catalogue. This was a working tool for the

Friends who were marshalling Fox's texts for publication after his death. It consists primarily of a quotation from the start sufficient to identify each text; these are arranged in the order of the date when written, and the place where they were written from is added, which served to establish Fox's movements and to show which of the gathered Meetings had benefited by his presence. A very valuable feature written into the end of the volume is a set of texts dictated by Fox when at the height of his powers. Very few of these have ever been published, and several are contained in this book.

It would seem that together this great collection comprises a probably unique record of the foundation and creation of any religious movement or Church.

A Note on the Editing

Especially in the earlier years Fox dictated as a young country man of his time might speak. It shows up for example in excessive use of the connective 'and' as well as the practice of putting the most important word at the finish of a the sentence. He used short words. Later he learnt a more literary—or to be frank more educated—style of expression. Nevertheless, we have to bear in mind all the time that these texts were produced orally, they are not literary constructions. It is this quality that permits us to say that through them, or at least through those that were not heavily edited, George Fox can speak for himself.

Fox himself did not refine the structure of his sentences or paragraphs as they flowed forth, and he was indifferent to niceties of grammar, punctuation, spelling and the use of capital letters. So too were his various amanuenses. Even when checking over the resultant transcribed versions, Fox did not bother with these matters. Therefore any of his texts that were printed had to be edited, in the case of the pamphlets probably by the printer himself, who is usually named. Thus it is the case that except for the manuscripts everything we have from Fox has been, and in fact has to be, edited. This editing by one person or another has been very variable, so much so that it has been said that Fox has suffered from his editors.

The greatest task of editing was undertaken by Thomas Ellwood in preparing the definitive volumes of the Journal, Epistles and Doctrinals. Nevertheless, his labours have come in for some knocks by contemporary workers, as shown in the Preface to John Nickalls' edition of the Journal, page x.

Early in this study much attention was given, in collaboration with Joseph Pickvance and others, as how best to present George Fox's texts for the modern general reader. Certainly the results have to be faithful to his intent, but it is desirable to make them more readily accessible by using contemporary idiom and structure of sentences. Many English words have changed their meanings in three hundred years—a very effective treatment of this aspect being given in Joseph Pickvance's *A Reader's Companion to George Fox's Journal*.[1] Nor is it helpful to have too many detailed indications of changes or omissions such as might delight an academic student.

Furthermore, whatever may be George Fox's qualities, admirable, endearing or otherwise, he greatly lacked discrimination about what to say or not to say to convey his main points—at least for the eyes of posterity. Therefore selection of quotations, and omission of

---

1   Pickvance, Joseph. 1989. *A Reader's Companion to George Fox's Journal*. London: Quaker Home Service. ISBN 0852452217.

redundant passages, are important for the modern reader.

The editing conventions used in this book fall close to those used by Joseph Pickvance.[2] Further, it may be said that some texts are given a more rigorously edited form, whereas others are treated liberally with the intention that they may best serve when read out aloud. The references to all the quotations are given precisely. If the reader wants to know just what the original texts comprise, there is no alternative but to go into the Library at Friends House, London, learn how to use its treasures, and himself find his own way through that jungle of riches.

---

2 Joseph Pickvance was the doyen of the group studying Fox's teachings at this time. As a Reader on the staff of Birmingham University he asserted an influence that ensured an academic integrity in the work.

George Fox
A Christian Mystic

Section One

George Fox's own record of his spiritual awakening

When familiarity had been gained with the styles of Fox's dictation, it was noticed that in the early part of his Journal some sections are in his mature style, and others in his early style. This led to an investigation, and it seems that Thomas Ellwood had a paper from Fox's maturity which he divided into at least two parts, and interleaved into it passages from the start of the Journal as originally dictated many years earlier. All printed versions have corresponded to this melange. The consequence is that the impact of the mature paper is lost, and misleading conclusions about the start of Fox's ministry drawn.

The first fifty pages or so of any printed version of the Journal are derived only from Ellwood's version, as explained in John Nickalls' introduction, pp. vii–xi. The relevant pages from the Spence MSS have been lost. Furthermore, the originals that Ellwood worked from have also been destroyed, in common with all other papers he used in preparing the three

1

great printed volumes. (Contrary to what is commonly thought, the Annual Catalogue shows Ellwood had a duplicate version, not what has become the Spence MSS; it would be entirely characteristic of Margaret Fell not to allow the original to go from Swarthmoor Hall, across the hazardous sands of Morecambe Bay, to Friends in London.)

Therefore, no trace has been found of the original of this text from Fox's maturity. There follows a hypothetical reconstruction of it. The actual words used are taken from Ellwood's edition with only light editing. As was his wont, Fox indulged in many digressions, his fertile mind and interest in biblical quotation often leading him off the main point; these have been edited out. Also, the layout of paragraphs has been changed somewhat, and sub-headings added, to assist the reader follow the developing account.

What we are then presented with is a first-hand record—Fox looking back from his old age to the momentous events and decisions of his youth—of a great soul coming to the ultimate mystical experience of spiritual enlightenment; and in going out into the world to share it with others. Any such is extremely rare.

The text from Fox's maturity

That all may know the dealings of the Lord with me, and the various exercises, trials and troubles through which he led me, in order to prepare and fit me for the work unto which he had appointed me, and thereby may be drawn to admire and glorify his infinite wisdom and goodness, I think fit briefly ... to mention how it was with me in my youth, and how the work of the Lord was begun, and gradually carried on in me, even from my childhood.

Childhood

I was born in the month called July, 1624, at Drayton-in-the-Clay, in Leicestershire. My father's name was Christopher Fox; he was by profession a weaver, an honest man; and there was a seed of God in him. The neighbours called him Righteous Christer. My mother was an upright woman; her maiden name was Mary Lago, of the family of the Lagos, and of the stock of the martyrs.

In my very young years I had a gravity and stayedness of mind and spirit, not usual in children; insomuch that when I saw old men behave lightly and wantonly towards each other, I had a dislike thereof raised in my heart, and said within myself "If ever I come to be a man, surely I shall not do so, nor be so wanton".

When I came to eleven years of age, I knew pureness and righteousness; for while a child I was taught how to walk to be kept pure. (Fox used the word *walk* with the meaning 'to behave'.) The Lord taught me to be faithful in all things, and to act faithfully two ways, viz. inwardly to God, and outwardly to man; and to keep to yea and nay in all things. For the Lord showed me that though the people of the world have mouths full of deceit and changeable words, yet I was to keep to yea and nay in all things; and that my words should be few and savoury, seasoned with grace; and that I might not eat and drink to make myself wanton, but for health, using the creatures in their service, as servants in their places, to the glory of Him that created them; they being in their covenant, and I being brought up into the covenant, as sanctified by the Word which was in the beginning, by which all things are upheld; wherein is unity with the creation.

But people being strangers to the covenant of life with God, they eat and drink to make themselves wanton with the creatures, wasting them upon their own lusts, and living in all filthiness, loving foul ways, and devouring the creation; and all this in the world, in the pollutions thereof, without God. Therefore I was to shun all such.

Afterwards, as I grew up, my relations thought to make me a priest; but others persuaded them to the contrary: whereupon I was put to a man, a shoemaker by trade, but who dealt in wool and was a grazier and sold cattle; and a great deal went through my hands. While I was with him, he was blessed; but after I left him he broke, and came to nothing. I never wronged man or woman in all that time; for the Lord's power was with me and over me to preserve me. While I was in that service, I used in my dealings the word verily, and it was a common saying among people who knew me "If George says verily, there is no altering him". When boys and rude people would laugh at me, I let them alone and went my way; but people had generally a love to me for my innocency and honesty.

As a youth

When I came towards nineteen years of age, being upon business at a fair, one of my cousins whose name was Bradford, a professor,* and having another professor with him, came to me and asked me to drink part of a jug of beer with them, and I, being thirsty went in with them—for I loved any that had a sense of good, or that sought after the Lord. When we had drunk each a glass, they began to drink healths, calling for more and agreeing together that he that would not drink should pay all. I was grieved that any who made profession of religion should do so. They grieved me very much, having never had such a thing put to me before by any sort of people; wherefore I rose up to go, and putting my hand in my pocket laid a groat on the table before them and said "If it be so, I will leave you". So I went away; and when I had done what business I had to do I returned home, but did not go to bed that night nor could I sleep, but sometimes walked up and down, and sometimes prayed, and called to the Lord who said unto me "You see how young people go together into vanity, and old people into the earth; you must forsake all, both young and old, and keep out of all, and be as a stranger to all".

* One who "professed" to a religious way of living.

On leaving home

Then at the command of God, on the ninth day of the seventh month 1643, I left my relations and broke off all familiarity or fellowship with young or old. I passed to Lutterworth where I stayed some time; and thence to Northampton where also I made some stay; then to Newport Pagnell whence, after I had stayed a while, I went to Barnet, in the fourth month called June in 1644. As I thus travelled through the country, professors took notice and sought to be acquainted with me; but I was afraid of them, for I was sensible that they did not possess what they professed.

Now during the time that I was at Barnet, a strong temptation to despair came over me. Then I saw how Christ was tempted, and mighty troubles I was in; sometimes I kept myself retired in my chamber, and often walked solitary in the Chase there, to wait upon the Lord. I wondered why these things should come to me; and I looked upon myself and said "Was I ever so before?" Then I thought, because I had forsaken my relations I had done amiss against them; so I was brought to call to mind all my time that I had spent, and to consider whether I had wronged any. But temptations grew more and more, and I was tempted almost to despair; and when Satan could not effect his design upon me that way, he laid snares for me, and baits to draw me to commit some sin, whereby he could take advantage to bring me to despair. I was about twenty years of age when these exercises came upon me. I continued in that condition some years, in great trouble, and fain would have put it from me. I went to many a priest to look for comfort, but found no comfort from them.

From Barnet I went to London, where I took a lodging, and was under great misery and trouble there; for I looked upon the great professors of the city and I saw all was dark and under the chain of darkness. I had an uncle there, one Pickering a baptist (and they were tender then), yet I could not impart my mind to him nor join with them; for I saw all, young and old, where they were. Some tender people would have had me stay, but I was fearful, and returned homewards into Leicester-shire again, having a regard upon my mind unto my parents and relations lest I should grieve them—who I understood were grieved at my absence.

When I was come down into Leicestershire, my relations would have had me marry, but I told them I was but a lad, and I must get wisdom. Others would have had me into the auxiliary band among the soldiery, but I refused; and I was grieved that they proffered such things to me, being a tender youth. Then I went to Coventry, where I took a chamber for a while at a professor's house, till people began to be acquainted with me—for there were many tender people in that town. After some time I went into my own country again, and was there about a year, in great sorrows and troubles and walked many nights by myself.

Seeking among the priests

Then the priest of Drayton, the town of my birth, whose name was Nathaniel Stevens, came often to me, and I went often to him; and another priest sometimes came with him; and they would give place to me to hear me, and I would ask them questions and reason with them. And this priest Stevens asked me a question, viz, Why Christ cried out upon the cross "My God, my God, why hast thou forsaken me?" and why he said "If it be possible, let this cup pass from me; yet not my will, but thine be done"? I told him that at that time the sins of all mankind were upon him, and their iniquities and transgressions with which he was wounded, which he was to bear and to be an offering for, as he was a man, but he died not as he was God ; and so, in that he dies for all men and tasted death for every man, he was an offering for the sins of the whole world. This I spoke, being at that time in a measure sensible of Christ's sufferings and what he went through. And the priest said "It was a very good, full answer, and such a one as he had not heard." At that time he would applaud and speak highly of me to others; and what I said in discourse to him on the week-days he would preach on the first-days, for which I did not like him. This priest afterwards became my great persecutor.

After this I went to another ancient priest at Mancetter, in Warwickshire, and reasoned with him about the ground of despair and temptations; but he was ignorant of my condition, he bade me take tobacco and sing psalms. Tobacco was a thing I did not love, and psalms I was not in a state to sing—I could not sing. Then he bade me come again and he would tell me many things; but when I came he was angry and pettish, for my former words had displeased him. He told my troubles, sorrows and griefs to his servants, so that it was got among the milk-lasses; it grieved me that I had opened my mind to such a one. I saw they were all miserable comforters; and this brought my troubles more upon me.

Then I heard of a priest living about Tamworth, who was accounted an experienced man, and I went to him; but I found him only like an empty hollow cask. I heard also of one called Dr Cradock, of Coventry, and went to him.… Now, as we were walking together in his garden, the alley being narrow I chanced, in turning, to set my foot on the side of a bed, at which the man was in such a rage as if his house had been on fire. Thus all our discourse was lost, and I went away in sorrow.…

After this I went to another, one Macham, a priest in high account. He would needs give me some physic, and I was to have them let blood; but they could not get one drop from me … my body being as it were dried up with sorrows, grief and troubles.…

When the time called Christmas came, while others were feasting and sporting themselves, I looked out poor widows from house to house, and gave them some money. When I was invited to marriages (as I sometimes was) I went to none at all, but the next day or soon after I would go and visit them, and if they were poor I gave them some money—for I had wherewith both to keep myself from being chargeable to others, and to administer something to the necessities of [those who were in need].

First openings

About the beginning of the year 1646, as I was going to Coventry and approaching towards the gate, a consideration arose in me, how it was said that "all Christians are believers, both protestants and papists"; and the Lord opened to me that, if all were believers, then they were all born of God, and passed from death to life, and that none were true believers but such; and though others said they were believers, yet they were not.

At another time, as I was walking in a field on a first-day morning, the Lord opened to me "that being bred at Oxford or Cambridge was not enough to fit and qualify men to be ministers of Christ"; and I wondered at it, because it was the common belief of people. But I saw it clearly as the Lord opened it to me, and was satisfied, and admired the goodness of the Lord who had opened this unto me that morning.

This struck at priest Stevens' ministry.... But my relations were much troubled that I would not go with them to hear the priests; for I would get myself into the orchards or the fields, with my bible by myself.... I saw that to be a true believer was another thing than they looked upon it to be.... What then should I follow such [priests] for?

So neither these nor any of the dissenting people could I join with, but was as a stranger to all, relying wholly upon the lord Jesus Christ.

Another time it was opened to me "That God, who made the world, did not dwell in temples made with hands". This at first seemed a strange word, because both priests and people used to call their temples or churches dreadful places, holy ground, and the temples of God. But the Lord showed me clearly that he did not dwell in these temples which men had commanded and set up, but in people's hearts....

My relations told me Stevens had been there and told them "he was afraid [for] me, for going after new lights". I smiled to myself, knowing what the Lord had opened to me concerning him and his brethren; ... But I brought them scriptures, and told them there was an anointing within each man to teach him, and that the Lord would teach his people himself.

I had also great openings concerning the things written in Revelations. When I spoke of them the priests and professors would say that was a sealed book and would have kept me out of it. But I told them Christ could open the seals, and that they were the nearest things to us: for the Epistles were written to the saints that lived in former ages but the Revelations were written of things to come.

Meeting with other seekers

After this I met with people that held women have no souls—adding (in light manner) no more than a goose. But I reproved them and told them that was not right, for Mary said "My soul does magnify the Lord, and my spirit has rejoiced in God my saviour."

Removing to another place, I came among people that relied much on dreams. I told them, except that they could distinguish between dream and dream, they would mash or confound all together. For there were three sorts of dreams: multitude of business sometimes caused dreams; and there were whisperings of Satan in man in the night-season; and there were speakings of God to man in dreams. But these people came out of these things, and at last became Friends.

Now although I had great openings, yet great trouble and temptation came many times upon me; so that when it was day I wished for night, and when it was night I wished for day. And by reason of the openings I had in my troubles, I could say as David said "Day unto day utters speech, and night unto night shows knowledge". When I had openings they answered one another, and answered the scriptures; for I had great openings of the scriptures; and when I was in troubles, one trouble also answered to another.

About the beginning of 1647 I was moved of the Lord to go into Derbyshire, where I met with some friendly people and had many discourses with them. Then passing further into the Peak Country, I met with more friendly people, and some with empty high notions. Travelling on through some parts of Leicestershire and into Nottinghamshire, I met with tender people, and a very tender woman whose name was Elizabeth Hooton; and with these I had some meetings and discourses. But my troubles continued, and I was often under great temptations. I fasted much, and walked abroad in solitary places many days, and often took my bible and went and sat in hollow trees and lonesome places till night came on; and frequently in the night walked mournfully about by myself. For I was a man of sorrows in the times of the first workings of the Lord in me.

During all this time I was never joined in profession of religion with any, but gave up myself to the Lord; having forsaken all evil company, and taken leave of father and mother and all other relations, and travelled up and down as a stranger upon the earth, which way the Lord inclined my heart; taking a chamber to myself in the town where I came, and tarrying sometimes a month more or less in a place, for I durst not stay long in any place—being afraid both of professor and profane—lest being a tender young man I should be hurt by conversing too much with either. For which reason I kept myself much as a stranger, seeking heavenly wisdom and getting knowledge from the Lord, and was brought off from outward things to rely wholly on the Lord alone.

First exaltations

Though my exercises and troubles were very great, yet they were not so continual that I had some intermissions, and was sometimes brought into such a heavenly joy that I thought I had been in Abraham's bosom. As I cannot declare the misery I was in it was so great and heavy upon me, so neither can I set forth the mercies of God unto me in all my misery. Oh! the everlasting love of God to my soul when I was in great distress; when my troubles and torments were great then was his love exceedingly great....

The great awakening

Now after I had received that opening from the Lord that "to be bred at Oxford or Cambridge was not sufficient to fit a man to be a minister of Christ", I regarded the priests less and looked more to the dissenting people. Among them I saw there was some tenderness; and many of them came afterwards to be convinced, for they had some openings.

But as I had forsaken all the priests, so I left the separate preachers also and those esteemed the most experienced people, for I saw there was none among them all who could speak to my condition. When all my hopes in them and in all men were gone, so that I had nothing outwardly to help me nor could tell what to do, then oh! then I heard a voice which said "There is one, even Christ Jesus, that can speak to thy condition"; and when I heard it my heart did leap for joy. Then the Lord let me see why there was none upon the earth that could speak to my condition, namely, that I might give him all the glory—for all are concluded under sin and shut up in unbelief, as I had been—that Jesus Christ might have the pre-eminence—who enlightens and gives grace and faith and power. Thus when God does work, who shall hinder it? And this I knew experimentally [by experience].

My desires after the Lord grew stronger, and zeal in the pure knowledge of God and of Christ alone—

without the help of any man, book or writing. For though I read the scriptures that spoke of Christ and of God, yet I knew him not but by revelation, as he that has the key did open, and as the father of life drew me to his son by his spirit. Then the Lord gently led me along, and let me see his love which was endless and eternal, surpassing all the knowledge that men have in the natural state or can obtain from history or books; and that love let me see myself, as I was without him. I was afraid of all company, for I saw them perfectly where they were.... I had not fellowship with any people, ... but with Christ who has the key and opened the door of light and life unto me. I was afraid of all carnal talk and talkers, for I could see nothing but corruptions and the life lay under the burden of corruptions.

When I myself was in the deep, under all shut up, I could not believe that I should ever overcome; my troubles, my sorrows, my temptations were so great that I thought many times I should have despaired, I was so tempted. But when Christ opened to me how he was tempted by the same devil, and overcame him and bruised his head, and that through him and his power, light, grace and spirit I should overcome also, I had confidence in him. So he it was that opened to me, when I was shut up and had no hope nor faith. Christ it was (who had enlightened me) that gave me his light to believe in; and gave me hope, which is himself, revealed himself in me, gave me his spirit and gave me his grace, which I found sufficient in the deeps and weakness. Thus, in the deepest miseries and in the greatest

15

sorrows and temptations that many times beset me, the Lord in his mercy did keep me.

Two thirsts

I found there were two thirsts in me—the one after the creatures to get help and strength there; and the other after the Lord, the creator, and his son Jesus Christ. I saw all the world could do me no good; if I had had a king's diet, palace and attendance, all would have been as nothing; for nothing gave me comfort but the Lord by his power. I saw professors, priests and people were whole and at ease in that condition which was my misery; and they loved that which I would have been rid of. But the Lord stayed my desires upon himself, from whom came my help, and my care was cast upon him alone....

Christ's power overcomes the devil

Again I heard a voice which said "You serpent, you seek to destroy the life, but cannot; for the sword which keeps the tree of life shall destroy you". So Christ the word of God, that bruised the head of the serpent the destroyer, preserved me; my inward mind being joined to his good seed.... This inward life sprung up in me to answer all the opposing professors and priests, and brought scriptures to my memory to refute them with.

At another time I saw the great love of God, and I was filled with admiration at the infinitude of it. I saw what

was cast out from God and what entered into God's
kingdom; and how by Jesus, the opener of the door with
his heavenly key, the entrance was given. I saw death,
how it had passed upon all men, and oppressed the seed
of God in man and in me; and how I came forth and what
the promise was to. Yet it was so with me that there
seemed to be two pleading in me; questionings arose in
my mind about gifts and prophecies; and I was tempted
again to despair as if I had sinned against the holy ghost.
I was in great perplexity and trouble for many days, yet
I gave up myself to the Lord still.

One day when I had been walking solitarily abroad and
was come home, I was taken up in the love of God so
that I could not but admire the greatness of his love.
While I was in that condition it was opened to me by the
eternal light and power, and I saw clearly therein "that
all was done, and to be done, in and by Christ; and how
he conquers and destroys this tempter the devil and all
his works, and is atop of him; and that all these troubles
were good for me and temptations for the trial of my
faith, which Christ had given me". The Lord opened me
[so] that I saw through all these troubles and
temptations. My living faith was raised, that I saw all was
done by Christ the life, and my belief was in him. When
at any time my condition was veiled, my secret belief
was stayed firm, and hope underneath held me as an
anchor at the bottom of the sea, and anchored my
immortal soul to its bishop, causing it to swim above the
sea, the world—where all the raging waves, foul
weather, tempests and tribulations are. But oh! then I
did see my troubles, trials and temptations more than

ever I had done. As the light appeared, all appeared that is out of the light—darkness, death, temptations, the unrighteous, the ungodly—all was manifest and seen in the light.

Spiritual discernment

After this a pure fire appeared in me: then I saw how he sat as a refiner's fire and as fuller's soap—then the spiritual discernment came to me, by which I did discern my own thoughts, groans and sighs; and what it was that veiled me, and what it was that opened me. In the light I found it to be [what] could not abide in the patience nor endure the fire, the groans of the flesh that could not give up to the will of God, that had veiled me; and [what] could not be patient in all trials, troubles, anguishes and perplexities, could not give up self to die by the cross the power of God, that the living and quickened might follow him; and that [what] would cloud and veil from the presence of Christ—[for] the sword of the spirit cuts down and must die—might not be kept alive.

I discerned the groans of the spirit, which opened me and made intercession for God.... By this spirit, in which the true sighing is, I saw over false sighings and groanings. By this invisible spirit I discerned all the false hearing, false seeing, false smelling which was atop, above the spirit, quenching and grieving it....

He that knows these things in the true spirit can witness them. The divine light of Christ manifests all things, the spiritual fire tries all things, and severs all things. Several things did I then see as the Lord opened them to me, for he showed me [what] can live in his holy refining fire, and [what] can live to God under his law. He made me sensible how the law and the prophets were until John, and how the least in the everlasting kingdom of God is greater than John.

The law of perfection

The pure and perfect law of God is over the flesh, to keep it, and its works which are not perfect, under; … and the perfect law of God answers the perfect principle of God in every one…. None knows the giver of this law but by the spirit of God, neither can any truly read it or hear its voice but by the spirit of God; he that can receive it, let him…. They that walk in the light come to the mountain of the house of God, established above all mountains, and to God's teaching who will teach them his ways. These things were opened to me in the light.

I saw also the mountains burning up and the rubbish, the rough and crooked ways and places made smooth and plain, that the Lord might come into his tabernacle. These things are to be found in man's heart. But to speak of these things being within seemed strange to the rough and crooked and mountainous ones…. I saw many talked of the law who had never known the law to be their schoolmaster; and many talked of the gospel of Christ who had never known life and immortality brought to light in them by it.…

19

[A long passage of teachings, that finishes with] These things are here mentioned and opened for information, exhortations and comfort to others, as the Lord opened them unto me in that day.

Here the major bifurcation by Ellwood takes place. In the Journal much narrative from Fox's early travels in his ministry are inserted, although, as will be seen, Fox was not yet ready for that.

Even so, it is apparent from the abrupt start of the following passage, Ellwood must have deleted something. What it was, and what was his motive can only be surmised.

The consummation

Now was I come up in spirit through the flaming sword, into the paradise of God. All things were new, and all the creation gave another smell unto me than before, beyond what words can utter. I knew nothing but pureness and innocency and righteousness, being renewed up into the image of God by Christ Jesus; so that I say that I was come up to the state of Adam which he was in before he fell. The creation was opened to me, and it was showed me how all things had their names given them according to their nature and [purpose]. I was at a stand in my mind, whether I should practise physic *[medicine]* for the good of mankind, seeing the nature and virtues of things were so opened to me by the Lord. But I was immediately taken up in spirit to see into another or more steadfast state than Adam's innocency, even into a state in Christ Jesus that should never fall. And the Lord showed me that such as were faithful to him, in the power and light of Christ, should come up into that state in which Adam was before he fell; in which admirable works of creation and the virtues thereof may be known, through the openings of the divine wisdom and power by which they were made.

Great things did the Lord lead me into, and wonderful depths were opened unto me, beyond what can by words be declared. But as people come into subjection to the spirit of God, and grow up in the image and power of the almighty, they may receive the word of wisdom that opens all things, and come to know the hidden unity in the eternal being.

[There followed a spurious connective passage by Ellwood.]

The three professions

While I was in the Vale of Beavor the Lord opened to me three things, relating to those three great professions in the world, physic, divinity (so called) and law. He showed me that the physicians and doctors of physic were out of the wisdom of God, by which the creatures were made; and so knew not their virtues.... He showed me that the priests were out of the true faith, which Christ is the author of.... He showed me also that the lawyers were out of the equity and out of the true justice, and out of the law of God.... And that these three ... ruled the world out of the wisdom, out of the faith, and out of the equity and law of God; the one

21

pretending the cure of the body, the other the cure of the soul, and the third the property of the people. But I saw they were all out of wisdom, out of the faith, and out of the equity and perfect law of God.

As the Lord opened these things unto me, I felt his power went forth over all, by which all might be reformed if they would receive and bow unto it. The priests might be reformed, and brought into the true faith which was the gift of God. The lawyers might be reformed, and brought into the law of God, which answers that of God, which is transgressed in everyone, and brings to love one's neighbour as himself. This lets man see [that] if he wrongs his neighbour he wrongs himself; and this teaches him to do unto others as he would they should do unto him. The physicians might be reformed, and brought into the wisdom of God by which all things were made and created; that they might receive the right knowledge of them and understand their virtues, which the word of wisdom by which they were made and are upheld has given them. Abundance was opened concerning these things....

I saw ... the greatest deceivers

Then I saw concerning the priests that, although they stood in deceit and acted by the dark power which both they and their people were kept under, yet they were not the greatest deceivers spoken of in the scriptures. But the Lord opened to me who the greatest deceivers were ...—likewise among the Christians such as should preach in Christ's name, and should work miracles, cast out devils and go as far as a Cain, a Korah, and a Balaam in the gospel times, these were and would be the great deceivers. They that could speak some experiences of Christ and God, but lived not in the life; these were they that led the world after them, who got the form of godliness but denied the power; who inwardly ravened from the spirit and brought people into the form, but persecuted them that were in the power as Cain did; and ran greedily after the error of Balaam through covetousness loving the wages of unrighteousness, as Balaam did. These ... have brought the world since the apostles' days to be like a sea.

And such as these, I saw, might deceive now, as they had in former ages; but it is impossible for them to deceive the elect who are chosen in Christ....

I saw ... the hypocrites

I saw the state of those, both priests and people, who in reading the scriptures cry out much against Cain, Esau, Judas and other wicked men of former times, ... but do not see the nature of [those] in themselves. These said it was they, they, they that were the bad people, putting it off from themselves; but when some of these came with the light and spirit of truth to see into themselves, then they came to say I, I, I, it is I myself that have been the Ishmael, the Esau, etc....

Thus I saw it was the fallen man that was got up into the scriptures and was finding fault with those before mentioned; with the backsliding jews calling them the sturdy oaks, and tall cedars, and fat bulls Basham, wild heifers, vipers, serpents, etc; and charging them that it was they that closed their eyes, stopped their ears, hardened their hearts and were of dull hearing. It was they that hated the light and rebelled against it; that quenched the spirit and vexed and grieved it; that walked despitefully against the spirit of grace and turned the grace of God into wantonness; and that it was they that resisted the holy ghost, that got the form of godliness, and turned against the power. They were the inwardly ravening wolves that had got the sheep's clothing, they were the wells without water, clouds without rain, and trees without fruit, etc. But when these, who were so much taken up with finding fault with others, and thought themselves clear from these things, came to look into themselves, and with the light of Christ thoroughly to search themselves, they might see enough of this in themselves; and then the cry could not be it is he or they, as before; but I and we [who] are found in these conditions.

I saw ... the scriptures

I saw also how people read the scriptures without a right sense of them, and without duly applying them to their own states. For when they read that death reigned from Adam to Moses, that the law and prophets were until John, and that the least in the kingdom is greater than John, they read these things and applied them to others but they did not turn in to find the truth of these things in themselves....

24

Thus I saw plainly that none could read Moses aright without Moses' spirit.... I saw how Moses received the pure law, that went over all transgressors; and how the clean beasts, which were figures and types, were offered up when the people were come into the righteous law that went over the first transgression. Both Moses and the prophets saw through the types and figures and beyond them, and saw Christ the great prophet that was come to fulfil them.

I saw that none could read John's words aright and with a true understanding of them, but in and with the same divine spirit by which John spoke them, and by his burning shining light which is sent from God....

Thus I saw it was an easy matter to say death reigned from Adam to Moses, and that the law and the prophets were until John, and that the least in the kingdom is greater than John; but none could know how death reigned from Adam to Moses etc but with the same holy spirit that Moses, the prophets and John were in. They could not know the spiritual meaning of Moses', the prophets' or John's words, nor see their path and travels—much less see through them and to the end of them into the kingdom—unless they had the spirit and light of Jesus; nor could they know the words of Christ and of his apostles without his spirit. But as man comes through by the spirit and power of God, to Christ who fulfils the types, shadows, promises and prophecies that were of him, and is led by the holy ghost into the truth and substance of the scriptures, sitting down in him who is the author and end of them—then they are read and understood with profit and great delight.

The image of perfection

Moreover, the lord God let me see—when I was brought up into his image in righteousness and holiness, and into the paradise of God—the state how Adam was made a living soul; and also the stature of Christ, the mystery that had been hid from ages and generations—which things are hard to be uttered and cannot be borne by many. For, of all the sects in Christendom (so called) that I discoursed withal, I found none that could bear to be told that any should come to Adam's perfection, into that image of God—that righteousness and holiness that Adam was in before he fell, to be clear and pure without sin as he was. Therefore how should they be able to bear being told that any should grow up to the measure of the stature of the fullness of Christ, when they cannot bear to hear that any should come whilst on earth into the same power and spirit that the prophets and apostles were in? Though it is a certain truth that none can understand their writings aright without the same spirit by which they were written.

Every man is enlightened

Now the Lord opened to me by his invisible power "that every man was enlightened by the divine light of Christ", and I saw it shine through all. And that they that believed in it came out of condemnation to the light of life, and became the children of it. But they that hated it and did not believe in it were condemned by it, though they made a profession of Christ.

This I saw in the pure openings of the light, without the help of any man; neither did I then know where to find it in the scriptures, though afterwards, searching the scriptures, I found it. For I saw in that light and spirit which was before the scriptures were given forth, and which led the holy men of God to give them forth, that all must come to that spirit if they would know God or Christ or the scriptures aright, which they that gave them forth were led and taught by.

But I observed a dullness and drowsy heaviness upon people, which I wondered at. For sometimes when I would set myself to sleep my mind went over all to the beginning, in that which is from everlasting to everlasting. I saw death was to pass over this sleepy heavy state; and I told people they must come to witness death to that sleepy heavy nature, and a cross to it in the power of God, that their minds and hearts might be on things above.

The command to go forth to others

On a certain time as I was walking in the fields the Lord said to me "Your name is written in the Lamb's book of life, which was before the foundation of the world"; and as the Lord spoke it I believed, and saw it in the new birth. Then some time after, the Lord commanded me to go abroad into the world, which was like a briery thorny wilderness. When I came, in the

Lord's mighty power with the word of life into the world, the world swelled and made a noise like the great raging waves of the sea. Priests and professors, magistrates and people, were all like a sea—when I came to proclaim the day of the Lord amongst them and to preach repentance to them.

I was sent to turn people from darkness to the light, that they might receive Christ Jesus; for, to as many as should receive him in his light, I saw that he would give power to become the sons of God—which I had obtained by receiving Christ.

I was to direct people to the spirit that gave forth the scriptures, by which they might be led into all truth and so up to Christ and God, as they had been who gave them forth.

I was to turn them to the grace of God, and to the truth in the heart which came by Jesus; that by this grace they might be taught—which would bring them salvation—that their hearts might be established by it and their words might be seasoned, and all might come to know their salvation nigh.

I saw that Christ had died for all men and was a proclamation for all; and enlightened all men and women with his divine and saving light; and that none could be a true believer but who believed in it.

I saw that the grace of God, which brings salvation, had appeared to all men, and that the manifestation of the spirit of God was given to every man, to profit withal.

These things I did not see by the help of man, nor by the letter (though they are written in the letter), but I saw them in the light of the lord Jesus Christ, and by his immediate spirit and power—as did the holy men of God by whom the holy scriptures were written....

I could speak much of these things, and many volumes might be written, but all would prove too short to set forth the infinite love, wisdom and power of God, in preparing, fitting and furnishing me for the service he had appointed me to—letting me see the depths of Satan on the one hand, and opening to me on the other hand the divine mysteries of his own everlasting kingdom.

I was to bring people off ...

Now when the lord God and his son Jesus Christ sent me forth into the world, to preach his everlasting gospel and kingdom, I was glad that I was commanded to turn people to that inward light, spirit and grace, by which all might know their salvation, and their way to God; even that divine spirit which would lead them into all truth, and which I infallibly knew would never deceive any.

But with and by this divine power and spirit of God, and the light of Jesus, I was to bring people off from all their [old] ways to Christ the new and living way. And from their churches, which men had made and gathered, to the church in God, the general assembly written in heaven which Christ is the head of. And off from the world's teachers made by men, to learn of Christ who is the way, the truth and the life, of whom the father said "This is my beloved son, hear him." And off from all the world's worships, to know the spirit of truth in the inward parts and to be led thereby; that in it they might worship the father of spirits who seeks such to worship him—which spirit they that worshipped not in, knew not what they worshipped.

I was to bring people off from all the world's religions, which are vain—that they might know the pure religion, might visit the fatherless, the widows and the strangers, and keep themselves from the spots of the world. Then there would not be so many beggars, the sight of whom often grieved my heart as it denoted so much hard-heartedness amongst them that professed the name of Christ.

I was to bring them off from all the world's fellowships, and prayings and singings, which stood in forms without power; that their fellowships might be in the holy ghost and in the eternal spirit of God; that they might pray in the holy ghost and sing in the spirit, and with the grace that comes by Jesus, making melody in their hearts to the Lord....

I was to bring people off from jewish ceremonies, and from heathenish fables, and from men's inventions and windy doctrines—by which they blew the people about this way and the other way, from sect to sect; and from all their beggarly rudiments, with their schools and colleges for making ministers of Christ, who are indeed ministers of their own making but not of Christ's; and from all their images and crosses, and sprinkling of infants, with all their holy days (so called) and all their vain traditions, which they had instituted since the apostles' days, which the Lord's power was against. In the dread and authority of which I was moved to declare against them all, and against all that preached [but] not freely, as being such as had not received freely from Christ.

The outward testimonies

Moreover, when the Lord sent me forth into the world, he forbade me to put off my hat to any, high or low; and I was required to thee and thou all men and women, without any respect to rich or poor, great or small. As I travelled up and down, I was not to bid people "good morrow" or "good evening"; neither might I bow nor scrape with my leg to anyone. This made the sects and professions to rage. But the Lord's power carried me over all to his glory, and many came to be turned to God in a little time; for the heavenly day of the Lord sprung from on high and broke forth apace, by the light of which many came to see where they were.

But oh! the rage that then was in the priests, magistrates, professors and people of all sorts—but especially in priests and professors! For although thou, to a single person, was according to their own learning, their accidence and grammar rules, and according to the bible, yet they could not bear to hear it. As to the hat-honour, because I could not put off my hat to them, it set them all into a rage. But the Lord showed me that it was an honour below, which he would lay in the dust and stain—an honour which proud flesh looked for, but sought not the honour which came from God only.... This is the honour which Christ will not receive, and which must be laid in the dust.

Oh! the rage and scorn, the heat and fury that arose! Oh! the blows, punchings, beatings and imprisonments that we underwent, for not putting off our hats to men!—for that soon tried all men's patience and sobriety—what it was. Some had their hats violently plucked off and thrown away so that they quite lost them. The bad language and evil usage we received on this account are hard to be expressed, besides the danger we were sometimes in of losing our lives for this matter—and that by the great professors of Christianity who thereby [evinced] that they were not true believers. Though it was but a small thing in the eye of man, yet a wonderful confusion it brought among all professors and priests; but, blessed be the Lord, many came to see the vanity of that custom of putting off the hat to men, and felt the weight of truth's testimony against it.

The witness to the world

About this time I was sorely exercised in going to their courts to cry for justice, and in speaking and writing to judges and justices to do justly; in warning such as kept public-houses for entertainment, that they should not let people have more drink than would do them good; and in testifying against their wakes or feasts, may-games, sports, plays and shows, which trained up people to vanity and looseness, and led them from the fear of God—the days they had set forth for holy-days were usually the times wherein they most dishonoured God by these things.

In fairs, also, and in markets, I was made to declare against their deceitful merchandise, cheating and cozening, warning all to deal justly, to speak the truth, to let their yea be yea, and their nay be nay; and to do unto others as they would have others do unto them; forewarning them of the great and terrible day of the Lord, which would come upon them all.

I was moved also to cry against all sorts of music, and against the mountebanks playing tricks upon their stages, for they burthened the pure life and stirred up people's minds to vanity.

I was much exercised, too, with school-masters and school-mistresses, warning them to teach their children sobriety in the fear of the Lord, that they might not be nursed and trained up in lightness, vanity and wantonness.

Likewise I was made to warn masters and mistresses, and fathers and mothers in private families, to take care that their children and servants might be trained up in the fear of the Lord; and that they themselves should be therein examples and patterns of sobriety and virtue to them. For I saw that as the jews were to teach their children the law of God and the old covenant and to train them up in it, and their servants—yea, the very strangers—were to keep the sabbath amongst them, and be circumcised, before they might eat of their sacrifices; so all Christians and all who made a profession of Christianity ought to train up their children and servants in the new covenant of light, Christ Jesus....

And all Christians ought to be circumcised by the spirit, which puts off the body of the sins of the flesh, that they may come to eat of the heavenly sacrifice, Christ Jesus, that true spiritual food, which none can rightly feed upon but they that are circumcised by the spirit.

Likewise I was exercised about the star-gazers, who drew people's minds from Christ the bright and morning star; and from the sun of righteousness, by whom the sun, the moon and stars and all things else were made—who is the wisdom of God and from whom the right knowledge of all things is received.

But the black earthly spirit of the priests wounded my life. When I heard the bell toll to call people together to the steeple-house it struck at my life—for it was just like a market bell to gather people together that the priest might set forth his ware to sell. Oh! the vast sums of money that are gotten by the trade they make of selling the scriptures and by their preaching, from the highest bishop to the lowest priest! What one trade else in the world is comparable to it?—notwithstanding the scriptures were given forth freely, and Christ commanded his ministers to preach freely, and the prophets and apostles denounced judgement against all covetous hirelings and diviners for money.

But in this free spirit of the lord Jesus was I sent forth to declare the word of life and reconciliation freely, that all might come up to Christ, who gives freely and who renews up into the image of God, which man and woman were in before they fell, that they might sit down in heavenly places in Christ Jesus.

There must have been a reason why Thomas Ellwood split this text as he did, and probably deleted some vital words. There

may be a clue: one of the earliest printed documents summarizes episodes when James Naylor, George Fox or a few others were brought before the magistrates. One such was Fox's first arrest, with the questioning before his imprisonment in Derby jail. When reading this, I suddenly saw, between the lines, a sense of profound indignation. Fox had had the experience recorded in the sections "The consummation" and "The image of perfection" above, had begun to share it with others, and was faced with imprisonment. For what? Blasphemy!

Fox later was several times falsely accused of blasphemy. But any frank statement of the ultimate mystical experience, when no distinction can be drawn between the divine and the ultimate being of the individual, has always led in Christian communities to condemnation—and all too often to the stake and fire.

The investigation on which this is based has also given a possible reconstruction (not included in this book) of the lost early pages of the Spence MSS. It is noteworthy that what is left picks up just after that event. So perhaps they were removed to prevent any valid accusation of blasphemy being levelled.

Fox later adjusted his message, from which Quakers have inherited "That of God in every man"—a spark of the divine. But what Fox experienced were the flames themselves, paradise and perfection. The censorship by Ellwood has left us thinking that Fox's great experience was to feel Christ speaking to him. But this reconstruction shows that his ultimate experience was greater, the awareness of the indwelling presence of God and Christ. Surely the response to one illuminated by such an experience can only be commitment, devotion and dedication.

Section Two

George Fox speaks for himself

This group of passages is mainly selected from the original printed papers published by George Fox, and now in the Library at Friends House, London. The grammar, spelling and punctuation are modernized, and any word that has been added or changed is shown in square brackets; otherwise, they are Fox's actual words.

The reader is reminded that Fox dictated almost all of what we now have. Therefore the meaning comes out best when read out aloud—even quietly to oneself.

This first passage is preceded by a note "Written from the mouth of George Fox as he spoke it forth" and was presumably taken down in shorthand and transcribed. It is dated 1653, only one year after Fox's great meeting on Firbank Fell which is generally regarded as the start of the Society of Friends.

And all you Friends who wait, in that which is pure itself, which cannot lie, which does not change, wait upon God—for God does not change. And let all flesh be silent before the Lord, that the life may speak in all. Then the mouth of the Lord is known, and God is exalted and glorified with his own work which he brings forth. And meet together there and everywhere, and mind that which gathers you, and wait on that which is pure—which gathers you out of the world's nature, disposition, conversation, churches, forms and customs; which will knit your hearts together up to God.

That which gathers you out of all this is the spirit of the Lord, and to gather you up to him who is the father of spirits—that you may be able to judge and discern and confound all the deceit of the world, and grow up to be as kings, and nothing to reign but what is life eternal.

And beware of speakings in the presence of the Lord, except your words are eternal life—the eternal word of God; else it does not profit, nor build up, nor edify. So God almighty be with you in all your meetings, that you may see him to be your head, king, and lord over all—to you all who are enlightened with the lights of the spirit. That is the light which shows you sin and evil, and your evil deeds and actings, and the deceit and false-heartedness; which will teach you holiness, walking in it; and bring you into unity; and will draw your mind up to God; and in it you will see more light. But hating the light—there is your condemnation.

(From Several letters written to the Saints of the Most High, 1654)

In this passage Fox shows how one's spiritual journey starts in a small way, and grows to bigger things—

For those with the light ... loving it and walking in it and waiting in it, power is given, and strength; and being obedient to it, and faithful in a little, you will grow up to be rulers over much....

(From This is to All People who Stumble at God's Commands, 1660)

Keep to that of God in you, which will lead you up to God, when you are still from your own thoughts and imaginations, and desires and counsels of your own hearts, and motions, and wills. When you will stand still from all these, waiting upon the Lord, your strength is renewed; he that waits upon the Lord feels his shepherd, and he shall not want....

(From An Epistle to All the People on the Earth, 1657. Republished in Doctrinals, p. 101; Works 4/132)

Wait all you captivated ones who lie in the [spiritual] prison for the eternal power of God to raise you up.... Reason not with flesh and blood ... take not counsel with that which lies in your bosom—for that draws you nearer to carnal things.... But everyone wait in the pure to guide you to God; then you will see the promise of God fulfilled in you, springs opened, and refreshment daily coming from the Lord....

(From News Coming Up Out of the North, Sounding Towards the South, 1654)

Concerning the Way

Further we say that Christ is our Way, who is the light that enlightens you and every one who comes into the world. That with it you may see him, the Way, and come to walk in the way of peace and light which is the Way of God, and which is the new and living Way which the Apostles were in....

(From Some Principles of the Elect People of God who in scorn are called Quakers, 1661)

And this new Covenant, this everlasting new Covenant, is witnessed in our days; and this new heart, and this pure heart, with which heart God is seen. God has put his Law in the minds of his people, and in their hearts has he written [it], with which they do know him, and [know] he is their God and they are his people. And these witness [that] which the Lord has spoken formerly—in the ages past by his prophets—[witness it] to be fulfilled and come to pass; for that which is the end for which the Scriptures were given forth—to be believed, fulfilled, read and practised....

(From The Second Covenant ... or the New Covenant of Light, Life and Peace, 1657. Republished in Doctrinals p. 121; Works 4/154)

39

Towards the latter part of his life, Fox worked for the recognition of the equality—at the spiritual level—of women with men. This little passage might sum up what we now call discipleship.

Dorcass was a disciple, who was a woman ... Women are to take up the cross daily, and follow Christ daily, as well as the men. And to be taught of him their prophet, and fed of him their shepherd, and counselled by him their counsellor, and sanctified and offered up by him their priest—who offered himself for all.

(From To All the Women's Meetings in the Restauration, 1673)

Fox considered that to belong to a spiritual community was an integral part of the spiritual life—

So that Christ Jesus may be head in all men and women, and every man and woman may act from him their holy head, life and salvation; and keep his heavenly peace in their church. And every living member believing in the light—which is the life in Christ—and so [be] grafted into him the fountain of life and the water of life. And that they may feel the living springs and the rivers springing up in them to eternal life, which are the living stones, the spiritual household, of which Christ is both head, rock and foundation. And

Christ is called the green tree, which never withers, in whom they are grafted by belief in the light, ... from whom they receive their heavenly nourishment....

Now every one of these living believers are members of the living church in God, which Christ is the head of. And every member of the church has an office, and so every member is serviceable in the body of his office, within the light which is over darkness.

(From An Epistle to be Read in the Men and Womens Meetings, 1677. Republished in Epistles 1698, No 344, p. 410; Works 8/141)

~~~

The milk of the word, which endures

The Apostle Peter writes to the Christian Jews scattered in Asia Minor—

Having purified your souls by your obedience to the truth for a sincere love of the brethren, love one another earnestly from the heart. You have been born anew, not of perishable seed but of imperishable, through the living and abiding word of God; for

All flesh is like grass
and all its glory like the flower of grass.
The grass withers, and the flower falls,
but the word of the Lord abides for ever.
That word is the good news which is preached to you.

So put away all malice and all guile and insincerity and envy and all slander. Like newborn babes, long for the sincere milk of the word, that by it you may grow up to salvation; for you have tasted the kindness of the Lord.

~~~

George Fox writes briefly to Friends in Bristol—

All my dear friends—folly and wickedness will have an end, but the word of the Lord will have no end—it endures for ever.

So feed upon the milk of the word, you babes, that you may live by that which comes from it—which does endure.

(1st Epistle of Peter, 1:22–2:3, from RSV but using the phrase "sincere milk of the word" from AV.

From Fox's Epistle No 160, 1658, p. 123; Works, 7/152)

~~~

The word cuts down deceit

In the letter to the Jewish Christians, known as Paul's Epistle to the Hebrews, the apostle writes—

For the word of God is living and powerful, sharper than any two-edged sword, piercing to the division of soul and spirit, of joints and marrow, and discerning the thoughts and intentions of the heart.

George Fox writes to Friends beyond the sea—

My dear hearts—Do your business faithfully, and fear not the amazement of men, you sons and daughters of Abraham. Trample upon all deceit, and keep over all that, in the dominion of God's power, above the world, answering that of God in all. Spare not any deceit.

Be faithful, and you will find and feel the word which is sharper than any two-edged sword to cut down deceit. And you will feel the blessing of the lord God with you.

And if the world's works lie like a wilderness, do not care for it and do not feel it matters, but do the work of the Lord faithfully. Then you will feel it prosper, answering that of God in every one.

So God almighty preserve you in his power.

(Hebrews 4:12, from RSV but with "powerful" from AV. From Fox's Epistle No 182, 1659, p. 140; Works, 7/171)

~~~

Counsel about Meetings[1]

Fox writes to the Friends of Plymouth Meeting, perhaps when that Meeting had been set up only a short time—

Friends—Keep your Meetings, that you may reign in the truth, and in the power spread it abroad.

---

1 In Quaker parlance the term "meeting" is sometimes used to mean an established congregation. In this book, when used in that sense it is spelled with a capital M.

Keep in the truth, that you may see and feel the Lord's presence amongst you. Be valiant for it upon the earth, and know one another in the power of it.

So the lord God almighty preserve you, in his power, to his glory.
(Epistle No 89, 1655, p. 77; Works, 7/97)

In the same year Fox writes to all Friends in their Meetings—

F riends—Meet together, waiting upon the Lord, that nothing but life may reign among you. And that you may grow up in the life, love and wisdom.

All wait in the measure of the grace of God, to guide your minds up to God.

And all Friends, I do lay it upon you to see that all your Meetings be kept in order.

So the lord God almighty keep you all to his glory, in his wisdom to himself. Amen
(Epistle No 88, p. 77, 1655; Works, 7/97)

Dwell in the seed

Fox uses the word "seed" to mean Christ. It also carries in it the symbolic meaning of those who have the promise of the word of God, and so by growing true to type may find themselves to be heirs to the kingdom of God. Fox writes—

A ll Friends, mind the light, and dwell in it—it will keep you atop of the world.

Mind the seed of God, and know it, and in it be content.

Dwell in the seed, which is the heir to the promise of life eternal, and dwell in the possession of that.

And in all your Meetings, and words, be faithful to the Lord, and to men; let this be your daily exercise.
(Epistle No 112, 1656, p. 91; Works, 7/113)

Again, towards the end of his life, he writes—

Dear friends—My desire is that all Friends may prize the mercies of the Lord, and live in humility, in his power which is over all. So that you may answer God's witness in all people, in his spirit and truth, in a righteous, godly life and behaviour.

Let not liberty lift them up, nor sufferings cast them down. But live in the seed of life, which no man can make higher or lower—for that is the heir of God's everlasting kingdom.

So in this seed, which is your sanctuary, God almighty keep you, in whom you have life and wisdom; thus wisdom may be justified of all her children, and they exercised in it, in this day of Christ. Amen.
(Fox's Epistle No 413, 1687, p. 554; Works 8/306. Fox said "conversations" rather than "behaviour".

"Love overcomes"

Towards the end of his life Fox writes to Friends thus—

Dear friends and brethren in Christ Jesus, whom the Lord by his eternal arm and power has preserved to this day—all walk in the power and spirit of God, which is over all, in love and unity.

For love overcomes, and builds up and unites all the members of Christ to him, the head. And love and charity never fails, but keeps the mind above all outward things, or strife about outward things; it is that which overcomes evil, and casts out all false fears; and it is of God, and unites all the hearts of his people together, in the heavenly joy, concord and unity.

And the love of God preserve you all, and settle and establish you in Christ Jesus, your life and salvation, in whom you have all peace with God.

And so, walk in him, that you may be ordered in his peaceable, heavenly wisdom, to the glory of God, and the comfort of one another.

(Epistle No 417, 1689, p. 555; Works 8/308)

The symbolism of George Fox

A man is brought up or led by Christ his leader into the image of God, into righteousness and holiness. Through this he has dominion over all that God made, subduing the earth, reigning over it as a king. He comes to God as he walks in righteousness, in truth, in the light and in the power of God. All things become new to him in Christ Jesus, who makes all things new.

He walks as under a curtain, and as in a garden; all things are sweet and pleasant to him, and every thing gives a sweet smell. The heavens above are garnished like a curtain with sun, moon and stars. And the earth under him is clothed with grass, trees and all sorts of herbs. So that he walks as in a garden under curtains.

But as a man has lost the righteousness and holiness, and the prince of darkness corrupts him, this is a sad walking. His sight, his smelling, his hearing, his sight of heavenly things are taken away; and so are invisible and immortal things, and eternal and divine things. This is a mystery and riddle to him, and therefore let all people consider what a doleful, sad condition they walk in.

Christ leads them to peace and joy and comfort. He that believes in the light sees the joy, the comfort, the paradise, the garden of God, the garden of pleasure. He sees how they walk under curtains, how God has garnished the heavens, and clothed the earth with grass and trees and herbs; how all the creatures stand in their places, keeping their unity. He sees the sun and moon in their courses, and the stars keeping the law of the covenant of God.

(A much shortened extract from manuscript 61E Aa, bound with the Annual Catalogue of George Fox's papers. Dictated in 1669. Like other such manuscripts, it may be surmised that this is a recollected form of ministry given by Fox in meeting for worship.)

The living God

In one of George Fox's letters to Friends in New England, Virginia and the Barbados, he gives counsel and encouragement, and urges them to go out amongst the heathens, and the Christians of the other churches, to proclaim the truth that they have experienced. Part of his letter contains this fine picture—

Keep your meetings, and dwell in the power of truth, and know it in one another, and be one in the light—that you may be kept in peace and love in the power of God, that you may know the mystery of the gospel.

All that you ever do, do in love, ... which edifies the body of Christ which is the church. So as any are moved to go among the heathen ... bring them to the power of God—to that God who is a living God....

He is the living God that clothes the earth with grass and herbs, and causes the trees to grow, and bring forth food for you. He makes the fishes of the sea to breathe and live, and makes the fowls of the air to breed, and causes the roe and the hind, and the creatures and all the beasts of the earth to bring forth, whereby they may be food for you.

He is the living God, that causes the stars to arise in the night, to give you light, and the moon to arise to be a light in the night. He is the living God that causes the sun to give warmth unto you, to nourish you when you are cold. He is the living God that causes the snow and frost to melt, and causes the rain to water the plants. He is the living God that made the heaven and the earth, and divided the great sea from the earth, and divided the light from the darkness, by which it is called day and the darkness night. He divided the great waters from the earth and gathered them together; which great waters he called the sea, and the dry land earth. He is to be worshipped who does this.

He is the living God, that gives unto you breath, and life, and strength, and gives unto you beasts and cattle whereby you may be fed and clothed. He is the living God, and he is to be worshipped....

(From Epistle No 292, 1672, p. 324; Works, 8/41.)

~~~

On finding the still centre

Jacob Boehme, the German mystic who died in the year Fox was born, wrote the following passage in his book The Way to Christ. The book is presented in the form of a dialogue between the master and his disciple; when the disciple asked how could he hear God speak in his inner self, the master replied—

When you stand still from the thinking of self; when both your intellect and will are quiet, and passive to the impressions of the eternal word and spirit; and when your soul is winged up, and above that which is temporal, the outward senses and the imagination— being locked up by holy abstraction—then the eternal hearing, seeing and speaking will be revealed to you.

So God hears and "sees through you", being now the organ of his spirit. And so God speaks in you, and whispers to your spirit, and your spirit hears his voice.

Blessed are you, therefore, if you stand still, [and still] the wheel of your imagination and senses. Forasmuch as hereby you may arrive at length to see all manner of divine sensations and heavenly communications.

(From "The Way to Christ" part iv, Supersensual Life, by Jacob Boehme, translated by William Law. Edited by Hugh Ross. We know that Fox had in his library some of the books of Jacob Boehme.)

To Friends, to stand still in trouble, and see the strength of the Lord

Early in his preaching career, George Fox writes this epistle to counsel Friends to stand still in the divine spirit. Then they will see themselves, see their troubles and find their release from them.

Friends—Whatever you are addicted to, the tempter will come in that thing. When he can trouble you, then he gets advantage over you, and then you are gone.

Stand still, in that which is pure. After, you see yourselves; and then mercy comes in. After you see your thoughts and the temptations, do not think, but submit—then power comes.

Stand still in that which shows and discovers, and then strength immediately comes.

Stand still in the light, and submit to it, and the other will be hushed and gone; and then content comes.

When temptations and troubles appear, sink down in that which is pure, and all will be hushed, and fly away. Your strength is to stand still; after, you see yourselves. Whatsoever you may see yourselves addicted to—temptations, corruption, uncleanness, etc—then you think you will never overcome. And earthly reason will tell you what you will lose.

Hearken not to that, but stand still in the light which shows them to you. Strength comes from the Lord, and then help comes in, by another way, contrary to your expectations.

Then you grow in peace, and no trouble shall move you. David fretted himself, and then he was still, and no trouble could move him. When your thoughts are out and about, then troubles move you.

Come and stay your minds upon that spirit which was before the letter; here you may learn to read the scriptures. If you will anything in your own minds, then you tempt God. But stand still in that power which brings peace.

(From Epistle No 10, 1652, p. 11; Works 7/20. This edited version is based primarily on the manuscript version, Swarthmoor MSS vol.vii, p. 164 (Friends House Library). Words added by Ellwood et al in the 1698 version have been retained where they seem helpful, but a change of meaning has been made; the manuscript permits either interpretation, it is a matter of punctuation.)

To Learn Silent Waiting

Fox used the word "to wait" also with its second meaning of to serve.

This is to all who would learn silent waiting upon the Lord, and silent meeting. For none shall ever come to God who is upon the earth, but as they come to that of God in them—the light, which Christ has enlightened them with. That is it which must guide everyone's mind up to God, to wait upon God to receive the spirit from God. So the spirit leads to wait upon God in silence, to receive from God. As many of the prophets and holy men of God, they often sat long waiting upon God; they said "blessed are all they whose minds are staid[1] upon God, they should[2] be kept in perfect peace"; and "my soul, wait upon God"; and "the meek inherits the blessing".

And so you will find more strength, [power][3], the [living] water of life, the mercy of the Lord, and the presence of the lord God, as you are still. Keep to that of God in you, to lead you up to God. When you are still from your own thoughts, imaginations, desires and counsels of your own hearts, motions and wills—when you stand single from all these, waiting upon the Lord, your strength is renewed. "He, waiting upon the Lord, feels his shepherd, and he shall not want."

That which is of God in everyone, is that which brings them to wait upon God in every particular, which brings them to unity, which joins their hearts together up to God. So as this moves, this is not to be quenched when it is moved to pray or speak—for there is the power of the Lord, this is the arm of the Lord, the dominion, the victory over death....

The light is the door, the light is the porter, who enlightens every man who comes into the world; [so] that all through the light may believe. And he that believes enters in to his rest, has ceased from his own works as God did from his; and he has the witness in himself.

---

1   are staid = hold firm.
2   1671 edition has 'shall'.
3   vertue.

He that is born [anew] of God overcomes the world, he does not make haste. Here he knows a silent meeting and waiting upon God, and knows all people upon the earth if they come to the light Christ Jesus has enlightened them with—their crowns must be laid at his feet, and their peace taken away from the earth. They must come into Christ—God's covenant of peace and of light [between]4 God and man. Then all [people]5 must be silent before the Lord, so the life of God comes to guide.

But all you that be in your own wisdom and in your own reason, you tell that silent waiting upon God is famine to you;6 it is [a]7 strange life to you to come to be silent, you must come into a new world. Now [you]8 must die in the silence, die from the wisdom, die from the knowledge, die from the reason, and die from the understanding.

So as [you yourself]9 come to feel that which brings [you]10 to wait upon God, [you]11 must die from the other. [It is this] that brings [you]12 to feel the power of an endless life, and [you] come to possess it. [By]13 a silent waiting upon God [you come]14 to receive the

4   with
5   flesh
6   sentence rearranged
7   the
8   that
9   thou
10   thee
11   and
12   thee
13   and
14   comes

wisdom from above (by which all things were made and created), and it gives an understanding and a reason which distinguish the [earthly man].[15] And [this][16] life of God in [you yourself],[17] which brings you to wait upon God, which gives [you][17] life, brings [you] to know God—and to know God is eternal life.

To you this is the word of the lord God.

(From "An Epistle to all the People on the Earth" (part 3), 1657, copied in "Several Papers given forth for the Spreading of Truth and Detection of Deceit", 1671. Also in Doctrinals, pp. 101–102; Works 4/131–133)

---

15 beast.
16 the
17 thee

From a great collection
of George Fox's manuscripts

Introduction

This group of texts is selected from a collection of manuscripts that Fox dictated mostly during 1669. A note states they were dictated to Edward Mann while staying at the home of John Rouse in Newington, London, one of his step-sons. Many may have remained in shorthand form for over 20 years until Fox's texts were being prepared for publication, when Edward Mann wrote them out in longhand into the back of the great volume called the Annual Catalogue of Fox's papers, in the Library of Friends House, London. This collection was originally 113 papers; 14 were published in his collected Epistles and Journal, but the remainder have never been printed, either in Fox's day or later, and have remained almost unknown.

It may be pondered how any man could have created over 100 papers of substantial spiritual and doctrinal content within a few days. One is forced to the conclusion that even Fox could not have done it, so that something quite different must have happened. Thus it may be surmised that as Fox walked or rode from place to place he often became open to the promptings of the spirit, and so came with heart and mind prepared to any Meeting. In response to some situation, or moved by the spirit in the silence of worship, he would then stand up to say something. Now, we know that he had a phenomenal memory, so probably it was possible for him to "re-present" what he had said in his dictation to Edward Mann.

This certainly would explain the distinctive tenor of the papers in this collection. And in the case of some, and specially judging from their form, their substance and content, it seems likely that they may even represent Fox's ministry in meetings for worship. That makes them a special treasure.

The papers included here were chosen to reveal certain sides of Fox's character which may be unfamiliar to us. They were all excluded by the worthy Friends of 1700 who had the task of deciding which of his papers were to be published.

George Fox lampoons the priests

A predominating element in many of the texts in this collection is criticism of the priests and the other churches. The content of these is neither welcome or relevant to us today (although those who would become involved in ecumenical matters well may learn of the basis of Fox's views), but their vitality, imaginativeness and tone throw much light onto his personality which is otherwise largely hidden from us.

For the first three texts quoted, only the opening parts are given; in each paper Fox goes on to develop his chosen themes in a serious manner. The others (except one) are quoted virtually complete.

All you priests and teachers, who complain and say that you have served seven years at the colleges, and that it has cost your parents a lot of money. And therefore when you have served your time, and come to set up your trade, why should you not have money now....

People who hear you and look upon you to be their teachers—it is better for them to serve seven years to you, and for you to teach them your whole seven arts and your knowledge of Christianity (such as it is) and divinity (such as it is), than for you to think you have people under you all their lifetime, to serve you.

Therefore people had better make a bargain with you: to serve you seven years to preach, and you to teach them. And some to give you 4 pence a year, and some who may be poor 3 pence, and some 5 pence, 6 pence, 7 pence or more, according as you make your bargain and indenture. And you to teach them, and at the end of seven years to let them be free men and women—not to keep them all their lifetime under your teaching, so that they may be always paying you....

And if you do not teach them your divinity and seven arts and your Christianity in seven years time, all people will shout at you "You are worse than any other tradesman, tanner, tailor or shopkeeper." For if they take a 'prentice, he serves them for seven years and is free at the seven years' end. For those shopkeepers were apprentices themselves, and cost their parents money, as your parents bestowed money on you.

And do you think that if the shopkeepers should not teach their apprentices their trade or art or function or occupation in seven years' time, then all the country would not shout at them and cry out against them? So as for you, if you should not teach them in seven years' time....

But if a baker or tanner or tailor or any other shop-keeper had served seven years, and cost their parents a great deal of money to learn the trade, and they should make you serve them all your lifetime, and force them to give you money whether you had their wares or not, or whether they had taught you the trade or not, what would you say of them?—but that they were the most unrighteous men in the world, and the most unjust men. And if you say so, what may they say to you? But weigh things with the true weight, and measure things with the true measure, and then judge yourselves, and see who are found to be light, or to come through the judgement....

(From manuscript Item 69.E, bound with Annual Catalogue)

Have not most of the public places of worship been like shops with distinctive[1] signs on top of them? And have not all these signs been from the pope, which is the cross? Do not you know your public shops by a public mark? Is not the sign of the pope's cross set on the top of them, where the priests and teachers sell their wares to people by the hour-glass—out of their public shops?

---

1   Fox said "nation".

Those of them that got uppermost keep their public shops, and then others who have their public shops taken away from them turn retailer-men. And are not both presbyterians and independents turned retailer-men, and do keep little shops? And do not they now get more money by their retail trade than when they were in the great public shops—with their sign on the top of them? And would any of you preach if you did not get money? You have laid aside Christ's doctrine and command—freely give and freely receive....

(From manuscript Item 86.E, bound with Annual Catalogue)

✺

All you pretended builders

In Fox's day the word "natural" was used with its meaning of existing physically, not enlightened or communicated by revelation. In the religious context it was therefore a term of criticism, meaning the very opposite of spiritual.

All you pretended builders of people up to heaven, who deny the light, deny Christ, deny God. They are all natural men. Their building will fall; their natural religion, and natural knowledge, and natural understanding with their own imaginations, with all their building, will fall down.

They build in the dark. Spiritual egyptians, spiritual sodomites and spiritual babylonians, with the jews, deny the light. And though the light may shine in their darkness, yet with the darkness they cannot comprehend the light. Oh! what a botchery piece of work have they and the jews all made in darkness! For how can they see to lay their timber, or to lay their stones, or to set their plummet? How can they build straight in the dark that cannot abide the light?

They would have none to believe in it, as Christ has taught—believe in the light, that you may become children of the light. For with the light you will see such builders. Yea, by the light the wise master builders will see God who is the builder and maker, and see Christ Jesus who builds up the fallen family of Adam, and builds up his house to God....

(From manuscript Item 73.E, bound with Annual Catalogue)

~~~

Who can make an image of God?

Who can make an image of an angel and who can make an image of the incomprehensible being that fills heaven and earth? For do you not picture up angels for a figure, and do you not make an image of God and set him in your bibles, both protestants and papists? Are not images forbidden by the law? And can you make an image of an angel or spirit, who can pass away in the fire, who are ministering spirits and flames of fire? Are you so bold to make images of them and hang them on your signposts at your taverns and alehouses? And to make an image of the incomprehensible God who cannot be comprehended? Heaven is his throne, the heaven of heavens is not able to contain him. And the earth is his footstool, [he] who fills heaven and earth, who is in all and through all and over all—God blessed for ever. Does not Moses convict you? who says—did you see an image, when the Lord spoke to him in the mount, for the mount smoked and was on fire.

Yet you in your darkness will go make an image of God, of the bigness of a corruptible man—when you are not able to comprehend him, the incomprehensible God, the omnipotent God, who is invisible and omnipotent, forbids you to make an image of him. And is there any image that you make but you do adore in your hearts or applaud or delight in? when all images are utterly forbidden to be made by the Lord, who is in all and over all. And all nations are but as the drop of a bucket before him, who measures the waters as in the hollow of his hand, and comprehends the dust of the earth as in a measure, etc. Yet silly man in his foolish imaginations will go make an image of him before whom all nations is but as the drop of a bucket. And you make images of God like yourselves. So you are not far degenerated by your foolishness and ignorance from the spirit and truth of him in your selves, in your own hearts, who is to be reverenced, honoured, worshipped, obeyed and served in all things, by his power and in his spirit.

Yet you poor silly creatures, empty of life or light or grace or truth which comes from the God of truth, to have your image makers make an image of him whom the heaven of heavens is not able to contain, the heaven also being his throne and the earth his footstool, and [who] fills the heaven and the earth. And yet you in your foolishness, darkness and ignorance go make an image of the incomprehensible God, and so you will comprehend him in the fashion of a man—for look in your bibles and there you may see your foolish ignorance and darkness and boldness, which is forbidden in the law of God to make any likeness of any thing either in heaven or earth.

(Manuscript Item 104.E, bound with Annual Catalogue)

⌇⌇

Old Cain was a fugitive and a vagabond

Now old Cain was a fugitive and a vagabond, who killed his brother and built a city opposite the city of God, which God's people in the old world were before....

The pope, his company and followers which are ravened from the voice of God and spirit, and kills his brother about religion and worship like old Cain. And has not he the old pope, Cain-like, ... set up his opposition ... to heavenly Jerusalem? ... And set up as head of his city ... in opposition to Christ and his church?...

Is not this young Cain a vagabond and fugitive?...

And the pope having lost the image of Christ sets up an outward image of him, and [has] lost the day of Christ and observes outward days.... Lost the true church and set up a wooden or stone one.... And made things of his own ... bread and wine ... schools and colleges ... crosses and images....

So he is a renegade and vagabond from truth, who has killed his brethren about religion like his old father

Cain. You see how his city is set up by this spirit, out of truth, in opposition to the spirit and to the city of the living God—the church of the living God which Christ is the head of, heavenly Jerusalem.

(Extracts from manuscript Item 123.E, bound with Annual Catalogue)

~~⌢~~

They that quench and vex the spirit

They that quench and vex and grieve the spirit, and hate the light, and turn the grace of God into wantonness in themselves, and trample the blood of the covenant under feet, make shipwrack of faith and of a good conscience. They would rule over the tender plants of God, over the grace of God in others, over the light in others, and make the garden of God as a wilderness; and [would] raise up storms and tempests against the tender blossoms, and so make war against the righteous; and would hinder the plant from growing and hinder the flowers from rising, and would hinder the sun from shining; they would hinder the day from dawning, and would hinder the day star from rising; they would hinder the springs from running and rivers from flowing as they imagine. All such as quench the spirit of God and grieve it in the[ir] own particulars and turn the grace of God into wantonness. No! among such is the throne of iniquity and the chair of the scornful and false judgement.

But do you think, [you] that grieve and quench the spirit, and that turn the grace of God into wantonness, do you think that you can hinder the outward day from falling, or do you think that you can hinder the pleasant showers from raining, or the outward sun from rising or the day star from appearing or day from dawning, or do you think you can keep it always winter or stop the summer from coming, and the tender herbs and fine flowers or the fruits of the trees from bringing forth?

Then you may say we will hinder the work of God and heavenly plant and the garden of God with all its plants from bringing forth fruits, and all the heavenly springs and all the heavenly showers and all the heavenly dews that fall upon the tender plants; or then we will hinder the heavenly sun and the heavenly stars, we will stop them in their courses. If you can stop the outward then you may say we will stop the heavenly; but poor vain man, you may labour in vain, [you] that grieve the spirit in yourselves, by which you should know the firmament of heaven with all the heavenly stars and heavenly sun and the heavenly day with the day star. For your thorns of iniquity is it not in the region of darkness, out of the region of light, [you] who quench and grieve and vex the spirit of God, [and] who by the spirit of God are judged and by the light are condemned?

(Manuscript Item 106.E, bound with Annual Catalogue)

Laymen and laywomen gave forth scripture

All you laymen and women—you know that laymen and women gave forth the scripture. And so let the laymen and laywomen minister forth their own scripture, and let the priests minister forth their scriptures and make their texts on them. And so you will see a difference, for the priests did give forth the worst scripture that were—as you may read in the bible—and pharisees, scribes and saducees; and the worst language that Christ had in the world it was from the priests and their disciples. And so the priests would have no laymen to meddle with scripture, for they would not have them to have spoken them forth, they would not have had Peter and John spoke forth scriptures, nor the prophets; and who are they that would not have Amos the herdsman spoke at the king's chapel? And so let not a priest take a text of the layman's words, Elisha a plowman, Amos a herdsman, Jacob a shepherd, Peter and John fishermen, Paul a tent-maker; but let them take a text out of their own priests' words that spoke so much against the prophets, Christ and the apostles. Let the laymen meddle with their own scripture and then there will soon be a difference put between the precious and the vile; and will you say that the priests were the vilest and most blasphemous upon the earth, and the laymen the best. And so it will be clearly seen a difference between the laymans' words and the priests great Rabbi's[?] words, for they were witnesses against Christ, and the laymen were witnesses for Christ.

(Manuscript Item 108.E, bound with Annual Catalogue)

~

All the people of God are God's plantation

All you believers in the light as Christ commanded, you in which you may see all the plants in the garden, and all the plantings of the Lord, and all the trees of righteousness which bear fruit [and] holiness— whose end is everlasting life, for he that believes has everlasting life.

And [you who are able] to see how pleasantly all the plants do grow, how they are watered with the water of life, how they are nourished with the dew and rain from heaven; and to see that all have water in their wells, and that everyone has bread in their own houses, and so that all your lights may shine and all your lamps may burn in your own temples. And all have salt in your selves, by which you may salt the earth, for it is savoury, it [needs] salting.

So none [are] to quench the spirit when it moves or stirs for God, in your own hearts. That none may despise prophecy—a prophet is a seer [when] his sight is opened by the light of the spirit of God; that none may despise it, and all may cherish it.

And all may encourage and help them forward, take the weak by the hand, and be eyes to the blind and legs to the lame, help the feeble knees, help the weary, drive on softly those who are with young. [So] stop not the springs, stop not the wells of water. But war against the philistines with the heavenly weapons, arm yourselves with the heavenly armour that you may war with the spiritual philistines who would stop up the well of life. None stop that which they have received from above, for it is not given to you only for yourselves—for no-one is to live to himself but live to God, from whom he has received, through Christ Jesus.

So come into the universal and general mind and general spirit, and to have the mind of Christ, the mind of the Lord—who would have all to be saved—to be tender of his plants that the Lord has planted, and of all his tender vines that bud and put forth. And with the shield of faith keep out the wild beasts, with the sword of the spirit keep out the swine and all wild creatures— for they are afraid of the sword and the fire—so that all the vines may be fruitful, and all plants may flourish and bring forth fruit to the glory of God; so that the Lord's lot may flourish and increase and bear and bring forth fruit to his praise and glory—who is over all, blessed for ever.

For all the people of God are God's plantation, household and husbandry, and [his] building and planting, and therefore [are the] fruits he looks for to his glory and to his honour and praise.

(Manuscript Item 109.E, bound with Annual Catalogue. Final paragraph omitted)

To have a fervent and sincere heart to God

A fervent heart is not a double heart, nor a corrupt heart. To be sincere to God and fervent in your heart, keep your heart single. A single heart, a single eye, the heart clean and pure, fervent against evil that would come in to the heart, against all deceit and guile and that which would make your heart unclean, or defile it.

In this fervent and sincere heart to God, the things of God are received, the love of God is received in the heart. For God delights in the fervent and sincere heart, [and those] who keep their hearts upright. Keep your heart upright, which God loves.

All unrighteousness, profaneness, unholiness, wickedness, and whatsoever would defile, is kept out of the fervent and sincere heart. It being kept out, there is room for that which is holy and divine to be received in the heart—for the pure and holy God. In the fervent and sincere heart towards the lord God, there is room for grace, and for faith, and Christ's blood, and for Christ to come and rule in your heart by faith. The things of God are precious and weighty; but by the corrupt heart they are slighted.

So the sincere and fervent heart will keep the heart from all vanity, up to the Lord whence life and substance comes, and [to receive] grace by which the heart is established. For whose hearts are established in [outward] meats, drinks and [holy] days, that is not grace. But where the heart is established in grace—not in meats—it comes of those things to Christ, by whom grace comes.

In the original this is a "thou" passage, Fox using the directed pronouns thee and thou throughout, which in his day had an added personal thrust.

(Manuscript Item 96.E Part 1, bound with Annual Catalogue)

~~~

George Fox on some roots of peace

An example of the use of symbolic phrases and images on a topic that is real to us—even "peace" being symbolically outward and inward.

All outward wars are in Adam in the fall, from their lust and strife and trouble and darkness and confusion; and [from] the many ways and worships and religions, teachers and churches and fellowships— strivings and warrings about them.

All peace is in the second Adam, the heavenly man, Christ Jesus, who never fell. Therefore, all must put off old Adam if they will put off strife and wars, and [must] come out of old Adam and their societies, ways, religions and worships [made by] men; [they must] leave the glory of [that]—for God has no glory amongst them in their work.

So all tossings and unsettlements are in Adam in the fall, and all stability and settlement and steadfastness is in Christ, the second Adam who never fell; in him there is no variableness nor shadow of change. He—to wit, Christ—was before old Adam was.

So if you would have life, you must come out of old Adam; if you would have peace, you must come out of Adam in the fall; if you would have life and joy and comfort everlasting, you must come out of Adam in the fall to the second Adam who never fell. If you will come out of woe and misery, you must come out of Adam in the fall, and put him off.

If you will have happiness and comfort you must come into Adam who never fell—Christ Jesus. If you will come out of the sandy foundations where men build their houses, you must come out of Adam in the fall— where the wind blows down their houses and the storm demolishes them. You must come to Christ who never fell, who is the rock, who is the life, where the house stands sure against all storms, tempests and weather.

[This is] where all the children of the light build their houses—in the light. They being believers in the light, they see the foundation to build their house upon, which is the rock, Christ the light. [They build] in the faith, in the righteousness, in the holiness, godliness, [power], purity and truth.

(Manuscript Item 56E Aa, bound with Annual Catalogue)

All you who call yourselves churches

Although this text was dictated, it should be visualized as a great peroration.

First, papists: You say that you never heard Christ's voice. How then were you married to Christ, [you] who never heard his voice, and Christ your husband never spoke to you? Strange kind of marriage!

And your husband never spoke to you, nor [you] heard his voice, and say it is a presumption to hear Christ's voice nowadays, and never heard the voice of the holy one.

Presbyterians: You say you are Christ's wife and spouse and bride, yet you say you never heard Christ's voice from heaven, and yet you will be married. How came you to be married and never heard his voice, and the bridegroom never spoke to you? How came you to be espoused? How come your contract by [one who] never heard the bridegroom's voice? Your saying so does not make you so—this manifests deceit.

And come independents and baptists: You say you are Christ's spouse and his bride and wife, yet you say you never heard Christ's voice from heaven. And yet you will be married. How come you to be married and espoused, yet never heard his voice? This is a strange thing. You have not the same power and spirit as the apostles had, who were married to Jesus Christ—that is the cry of you all. Can you be married to Christ without his spirit, without his light?

And all other sects that say you have not heard Christ's voice immediately from heaven, yet you will be his spouse and bride, and never know a time of spousing or contract or marriage, who never heard the voice of God. This manifests that you are not married clearly, but that you lie, and say not the truth. Persecutors were never married to Christ—that persecuting spirit, the first birth of the flesh. And so away with all your deceit, lies and falsehood, the whole refuge of them which you shelter under.

If any be married to Christ Jesus they must come to the light, to God's spirit and power, come to the truth in their inward parts which leads them to him, to Christ Jesus. And therefore you getting the apostles' and prophets' and Christ's words, and not being in the same holy ghost and power and spirit as they were in, that makes no marriage to Christ Jesus, but shows that you are degenerated from Christ and his life which the prophets and apostles were in, by which they were married to Christ Jesus, as they who are children of light and saints in light are in, who are married to Christ Jesus.

For Christ's spouse is now preparing for her husband. She has sought out her beloved, and gone to the watchman of the night and said to them "Did you see my beloved?"

You know that the papists were the watchmen of every parish not long since. Christ's beloved, who wandered up and down their city, said to the watchmen "Did you see my beloved?" They said "What is your beloved more than any other beloved? What is your religion, church or way, more than any other?"—thus signifying that another was their beloved. So they are espoused and married to another, and not to Christ. The spouse of Christ did not ask them for their beloved, for they knew they had not her beloved—she asked for her own beloved.

Then common-prayermen: They were the watchmen of every parish. She went to them to enquire of her beloved. These watchmen of the night wounded her—Christ's spouse—and sent her away, instead of telling her where she would find her beloved. And what did she get of the second, who cried "What is your beloved more than any other beloved?" For she knew that they had a beloved, but she asked for her own beloved, not for theirs.

Then the presbyterians: They were the watchmen of parishes when they got the power. The spouse of Christ went to the presbyterians' watchmen of their parishes and said "You watchmen of the night, did you see my beloved?" And they cried also—"What is your beloved more than any other beloved?" The presbyterians had got another beloved. The spouse of Christ did not ask for their beloved, she knew they had one of their own, which was not Christ's. So the presbyterians' watchmen fell a-smiting and wounding Christ's spouse, and so she went away wounded.

Then after, the independent perks up, and the baptists. They would be watchmen over parishes and peoples. So the spouse of Christ went to them and asked for her beloved. "What is your beloved?"—cry they—"more than any other beloved?" so signifying they had a beloved of their own which was not Christ's. And so the spouse of Christ cried "I do not ask you for your beloved, but for my beloved—you watchmen of the night." She wandered up and down, as she had the other cities. When they were the nightwatchmen and had the power, then they had their cities fenced with the powers of the night.... So they set a-wounding and striking at the spouse of Christ Jesus.

But she stands up and says "My beloved is fair, yea, the fairest of ten thousand of your beloveds. Set up ten thousand of your beloveds, my beloved is fairest of them all—Christ Jesus—for I am his spouse and bride. So my beloved is the fairest of them all, for my beloved never fell, he never dirtied his face, nor never changed nor dirtied his garments; his eyes are clear, and his locks and body complete. All your beloveds lie in the fall of old Adam, with his dirty garments, who has dirtied his face.

"How have you struck at my beloved? Who has gone about to mar his face more than any man's? Why do you make a trade of my beloved's words?—you watchmen of the night. For my beloved is mine, and I am his, who is the fairest of ten thousand, who was set up from everlasting to everlasting."

So now when the spouse had got a little past the watchmen of the night, she found her beloved, and so comes to the banqueting house, and the marriage of the lamb is known—glory to the highest, to the Lord who lives for evermore.

"So now I have found my beloved, he will order all your watchmen of the night who did smite me in your cities and wounded me when I was seeking my beloved. For how many people have come and asked you questions? How have you smote them and imprisoned them instead of answering them?—you watchmen of the night who pretend to watch for peoples' souls, and yet have not the same spirit the apostles had; ...

"But now my beloved I have found, and now is the bridegroom come, and the lamb's marriage is known. My husband will order all you watchmen of the night, I will leave you to him, to deal with you with his iron rod—for he has his heavenly sword on his thigh, is riding on his white horse through your cities; he who is king of kings and lord of lords, and has the greatest empire in the whole world—all power in heaven and earth is given to him."

His spouse is his empress clothed in white raiment and fine linen, the righteousness of the saints, the righteousness of Christ Jesus. This is the spouse of Christ clothed withal, who knows the voice of Christ, who hears his voice; who is bone of his bone, and flesh of his flesh; who has the mind of Christ Jesus her husband, who has his spirit. And he dwells with her, he who crowns his spouse, his bride and wife, with the crown of life; who has given her a new name, and the new white stone. She now comes to inherit all things, and has the right to the tree of life which, feeding upon it, lives forever; she has overcome, and shall no more go forth; she sees all who are without truth, without life, without a new name, without the new stone.

And so Christ and his spouse do live, to gather in the heavenly banqueting house with the heavenly wine and water and garments. The lord God almighty has his heavenly praise and his heavenly honour and his heavenly thanks—he who is blessed forever, from everlasting to everlasting.

And all the true worshippers in the spirit and truth are the spouse of Christ....

(Manuscript Item 119.E, Part 2, bound with Annual Catalogue)

The spirit of God

All people who retain God in their knowledge, they keep to the spirit of God which God pours upon all flesh—to wit, men and women. And also you must believe in the light, in the life of Christ, the word, which he enlightens them with; and bids them believe in the light.

They who go astray from the spirit of God and rebel against it, and hate the light of Christ and do not believe in it, they are not likely to retain God in their knowledge, nor the things of God, nor see them, nor know them, without his spirit and light.

For the light, as the apostle says, shines in the heart and gives the knowledge of the glory of God in the face of Christ Jesus to all the believers in it.

(Manuscript Item 15.38.G, Part 8, bound with Annual Catalogue)

Miracles of miracles

He is a quickening spirit, he is a physician of value, he is come among the dead in Adam and gives them life. If he makes some of those that are dead in Adam alive and quickens them, that's a miracle. If he makes them to savour or to taste, and to walk, here is more miracle. Are not these miracles, and great miracles, that Christ Jesus works? ... He does the works that no man can do or could do, for if they could he need not to [have] come.

So he it is that makes them to see heavenly things, and to see invisible and eternal things, which they could not do before when they were dead in Adam. He makes them to hear and to savour and to taste and to discover heavenly, spiritual, immortal and divine things, and invisible things. He makes them to walk—those that are dead in old Adam—to walk in the paths of the just, in the way of life, in the new covenant of Christ himself, who is the new and living way. So is not here a miracle of miracles?

So Christ opens old Adam's graves, he opens the pits wherein there has been no water, he removes the grave stones, he opens the prison doors though they be [of] brass or iron, he brings out of the jaws of death, he untangles the briars and brambles of old Adam, he sets the captive free, he binds up the broken hearted, and sets the prisoner at liberty, and the prisoner of hope sings for joy. Is not here a miracle of miracles?

Has not God appointed him to preach, when all those that are made alive by Christ Jesus, by the quickening spirit, they come to have the testimony of Jesus, which is the spirit of prophecy? "Prophecy is cease[d]" quoth the priests. "You are heretics that look for prophecy". Then you are all dead in Adam that have not prophecy, say the Quakers, [who] are made alive by Christ Jesus. For they that are made alive by Christ Jesus have the testimony of Christ Jesus—that's the spirit of prophecy. A prophet is a seer, and so with the spirit of Jesus—the spirit of prophecy—they see Jesus that has made them alive, and quickened them, and opened their eyes, and made them to speak heavenly things, and to discern and taste divine and immortal things. With the testimony of Jesus they see the law of death they were under, the pit, the prison, the thorns, the brambles they were in in old Adam.

So they can say by the testimony of Jesus: salvation is come and light shines and our life [has] appeared. By his light they see more light, and they can say by the testimony of Jesus who has made them alive: there is no salvation in any other name under the whole heavens but the name of Jesus, and his name is above every name, for the name Jesus signifies a saviour, Christ the anointed one of God, ...

Did they ever find life or were they ever quickened or were they ever made alive or had their eyes opened, or brought out of the jaws of death or brought out of the prison of old Adam but by the name of Jesus, the saviour?—and so made alive by him and quickened by him Christ Jesus. [Those] who have been dead in sins and trespasses, he makes them sit together in the heavenly places in Christ Jesus—signifying that they were scattered in Adam's graves, pits and thorns and prisons—but now made to sit together in the heavenly places in Christ Jesus, and now come to be gathered into the name of Jesus, where their salvation is, and not in[to] any other name in the whole heaven....

So gather in the name of Jesus where salvation is and life and redemption and mediatorship and peace with God is. To gather I say in his name, he is in the midst of them—for as Christ says where two or three are gathered in my name there am I in the midst of them. Then there is righteousness in the midst, there is light and truth in the midst, and a saviour and redeemer in the midst to comfort them that are gathered into his name, and to refresh them. So he is the head and they are the church, and there the head is in the midst of the church, ordering the body, ordering the church, ordering his sanctified ones and his spouse, his bride, his wife.

(Manuscript Item 52.E, 1663, bound with Annual Catalogue. This is initialled by G. F. An opening section may be missing)

⁓

Now is the Lord's everlasting light shining

Now is the Lord's everlasting light shining, and everlasting life and power shining over all the world, by which that of God in all must be answered. Now is the Lord bringing his lambs and his sheep out of the mouth of the beast and out of the mouths of the lion and out of the mouth of the wolf, and the wolf and the lion and the beast shall suffer hunger.

Now is the Lord bringing his lambs and his sheep out of the mouth of the beast and dragon and false prophet, that devour them and make a prey upon them, and have plucked the wool off the backs of th[ose] that have fled them, and have chopped their flesh almost to pieces as for the cauldron. Now is the great whore the false church losing her children.

Now is the Lord exalting his spouse, his bride, the lamb's wife his body his church, above all the world's bodies and churches. Now is the Lord exalting his house, which he will fill with glory above the world's house—for holiness becomes his house. Unholiness becomes the dragon's house, they plead for it to the death and grave, their unholy body for sin and death.

Now is the Lord's knowledge concerning the earth and waters that cover the sea, and now is the Lord exalting his new earth wherein dwells righteousness above the earth—where dwells unrighteousness. Now is the Lord exalting his virgins with oil in their lamps, that have kept their virginity, that has not been defiled with the man of sin. The marriage of the lamb is come—glory to God in the highest. Now is the Lord exalting his heaven above those heavens—which he will shake—setting his children in the heavenly places, making them sit together in the heavenly places in Christ Jesus, him by whom the world was made.

(Manuscript Item 67E, 1666, bound with Annual Catalogue)

Concerning all you that do cozen and cheat

Concerning all of you that do cozen, defraud and cheat, and oppress and wrong, and keep back that which is not your own and which is other's, that which you have gotten by defrauding or cheating or cozening or oppression or keeping back that which is none of your own from others.

That which you have gotten this way, it will corrupt, it will rust, it will canker all your whole substance that you have—that which you leave to your children behind you. It will corrupt [that], for by it your hearts and minds and spirits and tongues and hands are corrupted. It will bring you to beggary, and your children. And bring you to hell, for no defrauder, cheater, cozener shall enter into the kingdom of God that stands in righteousness and holiness. Therefore all illgotten goods, by whatsoever way illgotten, you make the poor and the needy to sigh, and the widowed and fatherless to groan; you make many pale faces and thin countenances by oppressing them....

But do justly, righteously, holily and truly, and keep to the equal measure and just weight in all things, in all dealings and tradings. Calling for righteousness keeps peace and truth, answers the good in all, and gives liberty. [It] does not oppress the good in any, but stands for equity and justice, and answers that equal principle in all, and restores every one to their right. What is gotten here never hurts any man, neither his body nor mind nor spirit nor his outward estate....

Therefore keep the law of faith, the law of love; do to all men as you would they should do to you. This is the royal law, royal measure, the true weight and balance. Keeping in this, you will honour God and glorify your maker, and live in that which judges all defrauders....

So know all people that God is honoured in the just weight and even balance, for he is just, and [is] dishonoured with the contrary. So all Friends, if you do not righteously, holily and truly, you will corrupt; for all injustice, unholiness and unrighteousness is out of truth—[it is] where corruption is, and cankering, and rust. Therefore keep in the righteousness, holiness, truth, justice, equity and faithfulness—that will keep you out of that which does corrupt, for it is over and above it.

(Manuscript Item 97.E, bound with Annual Catalogue)

George Fox on the Scriptures

To Friends, to sit under their own vine

This epistle would have been heard by Friends in the silence of worship.

My dear Friends, every one of you sit under your own vine, and there none shall make you afraid. In that you will bring forth fruit to God abundantly, to his praise.

As you abide in the vine, you will all become heirs of Christ and all come to know the seed, who is heir to the power of the world—where there is no end. And all come to be heirs of the kingdom, and so possess that.

And live in the seed—the top-stone—which was before enmity was, in which you will feel unity and power, and love and peace.

In that keep your meetings. G. F.
(Epistle No 84, 1655, p. 76; Works 7/94)

Here are some of the clues for that little epistle, which illustrates his intensive use of the scriptures—

Micah (4:1–4) tells how, when the nations have beaten their swords into ploughshears, every man shall sit under his vine. Jesus speaks of himself as the vine (John 15:1–11) and of his branches bringing forth much fruit.

Paul's letter to the Romans (8:2–17) and Matthew's Gospel (25:31–46) tell of the heirs, who shall inherit the kingdom. In the message from the angel to Mary (Luke 1: 26–33) there is to be no end to the kingdom of Christ.

The seed means Christ; it carries the figurative meaning of that begotten by God, the seed, offspring or descendants as in Genesis (17:1–18); it is seen by Paul as signifying Christ, (Galatians 3:16); together with the meaning of the word of God, as in Luke 8:4–15.

In Peter's first letter (2:2–10), based on Matthew 21:33–46, the corner-stone, once rejected, came to be the head or top of God's people.

It was the beginning that was before enmity was (Genesis 3), and in it was the Word (John 1:1–15).

<hr />

Fox on the gospel he proclaimed

In this passage, from an epistle written late in his life, Fox uses the word "seed" as meaning the spirit of Christ. He uses the phrase "Christ bruises the head of the serpent" with the meaning that it is this spirit of Christ that beats down the evil in man.

This is the gospel of God, preached to Abraham before Moses wrote his five books. It was preached in the apostles' days, and is now preached again. This gospel brings life and immortality to light, and it is the gospel of peace, life and salvation to every one who believes it....

This gospel was revealed by Jesus unto his apostles, who preached it. [Being revealed by Christ], it is not of man, nor from man. Now God and Christ has revealed the same gospel unto me, and to many others in this age.... In this gospel I have laboured, and do labour, so that all may come into this blessed seed, Christ, who bruises the head of the serpent; and that in it they may have peace with God.

This everlasting gospel is preached again to them who dwell upon the earth. They who believe it, and receive it, receive the blessing, the peace, the joy and comfort of it. They receive the stability in it, and the life and immortality which it brings to light in them and to them. Such can praise the everlasting God in his everlasting gospel.

(From Journal, 1688, pp. 585–586; Works, 2/336. Rather heavily edited.)

〜〽〜

Fox on the source of the scriptures

Fox wrote to Princess Elizabeth of the Palatinate, one of the states that are now northern Germany. She was a person of sensitivity and open mind—he says "It is indeed a great thing for a person of thy quality to have such a tender mind after the Lord and his precious truth." So he spoke openly and freely about his spiritual convictions. He spoke of the scriptures in the

following terms—(he uses a phrase "all christendom on heaps"
to refer to the churches being split up and at cross purposes).

And now, my friend, the holy men of God wrote the
scriptures as they were moved by the holy ghost. All
christendom are on heaps about those scriptures
because they are not led by the same holy ghost as those
were who gave forth the scriptures. Which holy ghost
they must come to in themselves, and be led by, if they
are to come into all the truth of the scriptures, and to
have the comfort of God, of Christ, and of them.

*(From Journal, 1677, p. 437; Works, 2/193. Rather much
edited.)*

~~~

Fox on the scriptures

The holy scriptures of truth are the truest history that
is upon the earth of the creation of God; of what
God has done himself, and what God has done by his
prophets and holy men and women; what God has done
by Christ his son, and what Christ has done by his
apostles; and what God and Christ has done from the
beginning of the world, in their times and fashions, and
what they will do to the end of the world.

And the scriptures—some of them are history done in
their times when they were written, and some of them
are shadows and figurative and typical of things in their
times—of which Christ is the substance and end.

So the scriptures of truth is the best book upon the
earth to be read, believed, fulfilled and practised. And

Christ the substance of them, is to be enjoyed and walked in....

Holy men of God spake them forth as they were moved by the holy ghost. So it is the holy ghost that leads into all the truth of them, in both the old and the new testaments....

No man knows the things of God but by the spirit of God, for it reveals them....

(From tract "The True Christians Distinguished", third part titled "Concerning the Holy Scriptures of Truth", 1689, Smith's Cat. p. 688. Thompson Box 31)

~~~

A stern warning

Parts of an epistle by Fox that clearly shows his view that it is the counsel of God that gave forth the scriptures, and the light of Christ that opens their spiritual truths to us. He criticizes those who speak from their own minds, even though dressed up in the words of scripture, and gives a stern warning to each one of us lest we speak out of—that is, without, or outside of—the light that comes from the true centre.

Friends, I do warn you in the presence of the living God, not to speak the things of God out of the fear of God, at random, in a presumptuous mind. For proud boasters are excluded out of the kingdom of God, and are condemned with the light of Christ; and with the life that gave forth the scriptures they are judged.

Therefore this is the word of the Lord—wait in the light which Christ has enlightened you with, and love it, and you shall have the light of life. It will bring you to stand in the counsel of God, and keep you from all wicked ways. With it, you will see all the enchanters, false prophets, who speak a divination of their own brains....

They who gave forth the scriptures were in the counsel of God; they were in the life of the scriptures, from which life and letter did proceed. Therefore every one of you (in your measures) wait and walk in the life, which gave forth the scriptures, and which will open them to you again. Else you all I do deny, and you are to be turned away from, as having the form but not the power....

I charge every one of you in the presence of the living God to take heed of the light. Loving it, it is your teacher; hating it, it is your condemnation.

(From Epistle No 34, 1653, p. 30; Works, 7/41)

Fox builds a mighty tower from biblical quotations

Friends—Stand still and see, be still and hear, sit at Jesus' feet, and choose the better thing. To do the work of God is to believe in his son Jesus Christ, the light. Your hope and faith are to stand in God, and in his son. Walk by that faith which he is the author of, and walk in the light, and walk in the spirit. As every one has received Christ, so walk in him, and so serve God in the spirit, and worship him in the spirit and in the truth—for God is not worshipped out of the truth.

The babes' milk is from the word, and their bread is from above, and there is no true religion but what is pure from above. And the stayed, patient people abide in their own homes....

There is no true church but where Christ exercises his offices in and amongst them, and they are asking their husband at home, and he is their head, and the true marriage to Christ the heavenly man is witnessed by such as are flesh of his flesh, and bone of his bone.

None come to be children of the light but such as believe in the light.

No sons of God, but by receiving Christ, and by being led by his spirit.

No coming into all truth, but by being led by the spirit of truth.

No running the true race in the straight way to get to the glorious crown, but with patience.

No purifying, but by coming to Christ, the hope of glory, the purifier.

And no overcoming, but by believing in Christ the light, and he who does so is born of God.

There is no true witness within but the light, and life and spirit of Christ, the true record.

No true faith but that which Christ is the author of, which gives victory.

No true anchor to the immortal soul but by Christ, the hope of glory—so by hope you are saved.

No true liberty but in Christ, and in his law of the spirit of life, and in his gospel.

No true knowledge of God, but by his light and spirit in the heart.

No salvation, but by the name of Jesus.

No true praying, but in the spirit.

No true singing, but in the spirit.

No true fast, but that which breaks the bond of iniquity.

No true fellowship, but in the pure faith, light, spirit, and gospel of God and Christ.

No true foundation, but Christ, to build upon.

No true way, but Christ.

No true seed, but what Christ has sown in the heart.

No true rest, but in Christ.

No true peace, but in Christ.

No true service to God and Christ, but in the newness of life.

No knowing things of God and Christ, but by the spirit of God.

No knowing the son nor the Father, but by the revelation of the holy spirit.

No knowing the scriptures, but by the same holy ghost that moved the holy men to give them forth.

No calling Jesus "Lord", but by the holy ghost, by which he was conceived.

No grafting into Christ, but by believing in the light, which is called the light in men, and the life in him.

No true wisdom, but from above; and no true receiving it, but in the fear of the lord.

No true understanding of spiritual things, but what Christ gives.

No divine reason, but in the faith which Christ is the author of—which gives victory over that which is unreasonable, and separates from God.

And no true love to God, but what he sheds abroad in the heart.

To know the fellowship with Christ in his death and sufferings is above the fellowship of bread and wine, which will have an end; but the fellowship in the gospel and holy spirit has no end.

(Epistle No 230, 1663, p. 201; Works, 7/243)

Section Three

George Fox on the meeting for worship, and ministry

Introduction

Meeting for Worship is for many Friends the most treasured part of their Quaker faith and practice. It often seems to be the element that draws newcomers to the Society of Friends.

When George Fox, after groping as a young man for years in the wilderness, had his great spiritual revelation—which he put into the kind of words that countless other Christians throughout the centuries might have used—"there is one, even Christ Jesus, that can speak to your condition, my heart did leap for joy"—he set about trying to help others to find a similar experience. He did this by travelling round the country, and preaching a message.

When Fox went to any place and preached his message, and found people responding to it, he urged them to gather together and set up a Meeting, to worship silently. He would go on his way, but sought to guide, help and exhort these gathered groups by writing to them. These writings serve as the basis for almost all the passages here printed.

We shall see Fox giving advice and counsel on the setting up of Meetings; and what he sees as part of the aim or objective of worship and how we can orient ourselves towards it. It may be of interest in this day of gender equality to see him trying to attain some opportunities for women. And spoken ministry— arising out of the silent worship—being such an important part of our Quaker way, he gives advice on that; and then we see his strongly worded cautionary warnings when things go awry.

The chief element in the primary message Fox preached relates to Christ. This is, nowadays, a difficult word for many of us, but Fox uses it, and we cannot escape from using it too. Fox made it somewhat easier by also using the word "light", and he almost always means the light of Christ. Here we have to allow Fox to use these terms without more ado.

The following passage speaks of something we know of from our own experience—the peace and quietening of the inner being that comes through meeting for worship. Fox first draws a contrast with the people of worldly ways or of the other churches, who are bustling and in strife with one another.

So there are all the unquieted spirits in the world, and the restless and the wearied. For there is none upon the earth that come to have their spirits quieted but [those] who come to the light, that Christ Jesus has enlightened them with. So here every spirit comes to have a particular satisfaction and quietness in his own mind, and here the weary come to have rest in Christ....

Such shall find mercy of God, when their minds are guided up unto God, and their spirits and minds are quieted in silent waiting upon God. In one half hour [they] have more peace and satisfaction than they have had from all other teachers of the world all their lifetime. Here they come to feel that which quiets their minds to God, and they find and feel the way of peace. [They] come to grow up in that life the scriptures were given forth from, the life the saints lived in and [the] spirit which guided their minds up to God, the father of spirits....

So as you all come to be guided with that of God within you, and to feel that of God in you to guide your minds up to God, you shall come to satisfaction—it leads you up out of the earth to that within ... and here the glory of the lord God comes to be revealed to you.

("An Epistle to All the People on the Earth", 1657, second part commencing "That which brings you to look...", Smith's Cat. p. 654; Doctrinals p. 96; Works 4/125)

◠◠

Setting up of Meetings

In the early years Fox gave specific advice on the setting up of meetings for worship. Here is the first part of a general epistle, again of 1652.

All Friends, who are grown up in the life and power of the truth, see that when you appoint your Meetings in any open place—in the fields, on the moors or on the mountains—that none appoint Meetings in your own wills. For that lets in the wills of the world upon the life of Friends, and so you come to suffer by the world. But at such Meetings let the wisdom of God guide you; that some may be there to preserve the truth from suffering by the world, that all burdens may be kept off and taken away. So you will grow pure and strong....

(Epistle No 14, 1652, p. 13; Works 7/22)

Near the end of his life, Fox wrote a memorial to the life of John Audland. Audland had been one of those convinced by Fox during the great sermon on Firbank Fell in Westmorland, in 1652—generally regarded as the start of the Society of Friends. When Fox wrote this and it was printed, it was the first published record of the Firbank Fell occasion. (The other record of it, easily read in his Journal (Nickalls pp. 108–109), was written earlier but not published until after his death.)

In this quotation Fox expands the theme we have already seen, but then—very characteristically—transforms it into something of greater significance.

When George Fox came to Firbank chapel in Westmorland, John Audland and Francis Howgill were preaching there in the morning...

In the afternoon there was a great gathering of people, more than in the morning, and so the house would not hold them. So I was moved to go upon a mountain hard by. The people gathered to the mountain, and sat down, though it was a strange thing to have Meetings anywhere but in the church, so called, because [that] was holy ground they thought—people were so ignorant then.

So after some time I stood up, and said unto them, That the ground was as holy as any other, and that Christ did meet upon a mountain, and by the seaside, and in houses—and so did his apostles and disciples. Although the Jews had a temple called holy, in the old testament, and a worship there, yet Christ had ended that temple and worship, and set up a worship in spirit and truth. All the true believers in Christ—who received him and his gospel of life and salvation—were the true Christians, and their bodies were the temples of God and Christ and the holy ghost....

("The Testimony of George Fox concerning our dear Friends and brethren John Audland and John Camm" from volume "Camm and Audland's Writings", 1689)

In the middle of his career—when the Quaker movement had become well established—in a long epistle that has a major section on worship, Fox expands the theme of the temple within.

We say every man and woman must come into the temple, if he worship God in spirit and truth. Is not the spirit within and the truth in the inward parts? For do you not know that your bodies are the temples of the holy ghost, which is the holy spirit?

Can any worship God—who is a spirit—in the truth, but [that] they must come to the spirit and truth of God in their own hearts?

Here we set up the public and temple worship, which Christ set up, which every man and woman must come to—truth in the inward parts and the spirit of God within them—[to] worship in the spirit. They must be in it, and in the truth, to worship the God of all truth—who is a spirit.

This is the public and universal worship; this brings every man and woman to truth, and [to] the spirit of God in their own hearts. So this brings all to know their bodies to be the temples of the holy spirit, in which they worship....

(Epistle No 249, 1667, p. 236; Works 7/292)

∿

From small things, larger grow

Three short quotations, the first from an epistle to Friends at Kendal when that Meeting may have been set up only a few months.

To that of God in you I speak, that you may watch over the weak, and see how the plants of the Lord grow. Walk in the joy and love of the truth, serving God with joyfulness of heart. To you this is the word of the Lord....

(Epistle No 21, 1652, p. 19; Works 7/29)

∿

[To those] with the light ... loving it and walking in it and waiting in it, power is given, and strength.

Being obedient to it, and faithful in a little, you will grow up to be rulers over much....

(Tract, "This is to All People who Stumble at God's Commands", 1660; Smith's Cat. p. 662)

~~~

O h! wait, wait upon the living God to nourish the tender plant in you, that you may bring forth fruits of righteousness unto God—for he accepts such, and none else. Therefore wait upon God, he has a pure seed among you....

(Epistle No 44, 1653, p. 40; Works 7/53)

~~~

Dwell in love and unity, sing in the spirit

F riends—... Dwell in love and unity with one another, and know one another in the power of an endless life, which does not change....

All Friends everywhere be faithful in the life and power of God. Keep your Meetings ... in that which changes not, [so] that nothing but Christ may reign among you—in the power of God, the wisdom of God, the sanctification and redemption. [So] the just may reign over all, and seed of God have the dominion in you all. With that you may all be ordered to the glory of God, and kept in the bond of peace, and reign in the love of God....

Have this love abroad in all your hearts, and feel it abiding in you—this love of God edifies you. Know the word of God abiding in you, which was in the beginning, and brings to the beginning. [This] word being ingrafted, at saves the soul, and hammers down, throws out and burns up that which wars against it.

(Epistle No 23, 1653, p. 20; Works 7/30)

My dear Friends, dwell in the everlasting seed of God, in which you all will feel life eternal, that never has an end. In that meet, and keep your Meetings.

Dwell together in the love and life of God: with [it] you may all be filled; through [its] love you may cover the multitude of sins, and answer the life of God in all; in [it] you may feel the blessings of almighty God covering you as a garment.

So live in the possession of the life—in which you all will have unity and fellowship with God, and one with another....

(Epistle No 120, 1656, p. 93; Works 7/30)

My dear Friends—Be not carried away by good words and fair speeches, nor the affectionate part, which is taken with them. But everyone have hold of the truth in yourselves, and the light, and life and power of the most high—by which you may be stayed on Christ, your bread of life. He is the staff of your heavenly and eternal life—bread is the staff of life.

Now friends, who have denied the world's songs and singing, sing in the spirit, and with grace, making melody to the Lord in your hearts. And you having denied the world's formal praying, pray always in the spirit, and watch in it. And you that have denied the world's giving of thanks, and their saying of grace, ... in everything give thanks to the Lord, through Jesus Christ.

And you that have denied the world's praising [of] God with their lips, ... always praise the Lord night and day.... And you that have denied the world's fastings, and their hanging down the heads like a bulrush for a day, ... keep the fast of the Lord—that breaks the bond of iniquity, and lets the oppressed go free.

[Thus] your health may grow, and your light may shine as the morning.

(Epistle No 167, 1658, p. 126; Works 7/155)

~~~

Stand still, wait, in the light

Fox uses the word "world" as we would use worldly, with a negative or dark meaning; he also uses it for those who have not seen the light. He uses "nature" in our sense of it being natural for a fish to swim in the sea. In the following passage "prison" means spiritual darkness.

For the first step of peace is to stand still in the light—which discovers things contrary to it—for power and strength to stand against that nature which the light discovers. Here grace grows, here is God alone glorified and exalted, and the unknown truth— unknown to the world—made manifest; [this] draws up

101

that which lies in the prison, and refreshes it in time, up to God, out of time, through time.

(Tract "That All would know the Way to the Kingdom", 1653; Smith's Cat. p. 645; Doctrinals p. 3; Works 4/17–18)

To Friends in Worcester

Friends—Every one of you, having the light from the son of God, wait in it. [Thus] you may come to receive the son of God—from whence it comes—[and] receive power from him to become the sons of God.

[Thus you may] have faith in him. For who are of faith are Abraham's seed [a] faith [that] gives the victory over the world. It is by faith our hearts are purified.

So dwell in the light that casts out all jangling spirits. [In that light] you may have unity with one another, and with Christ from whence the light comes; and [have unity] with the Father, whom he is the way to. With that light you may answer the light in every man, ... though they hate it. So the lord God almighty keep you and preserve you.

All keep your Meetings in the power of God, that you may see the Lord present among you.

(Epistle No 170, 1658, p. 129; Works 7/158)

All friends, meet together in the light, that with it you may see the father of life amongst you in your

Meetings. And so, the lord God of power be with you, and keep you....

All live in peace, in love, in life, and in the power of the lord God. Keep your Meetings, every one of you waiting upon him in the power of God ... that in it you may have unity with God, the father, and the son, and one with another.

Dear Friends, let wisdom guide you in patience, and do not strive with any in Meetings; but dwell in the power of the lord God, which can bear and suffer all things. Make no strife among Friends, but live in that which makes for peace and love and life, in which edification is known.

(Epistle No 66, 1654, p. 62; Works 7/79)

~~~

Wait in the power, that it may grow to wisdom

Friends—Meet together, waiting on the Lord, that nothing but the life may reign in you; and that in life, love and wisdom you may grow up. All wait in the measure of the grace of God, to guide your minds up to God.

All Friends, I do lay it upon you to see that all your Meetings are kept in order.

So the lord God almighty keep you all to his glory, in his wisdom, to himself. Amen.

(To be read among all Friends at their Meetings)
(Epistle No 88, 1655, p. 77; Works 7/97)

My Dear Friends, keep your Meetings, and you will feel the seed to arise, though never a word is spoken amongst you. Be faithful, that you may answer that of God in every one. Do not neglect your talents, but live in the life and power of God, which you have received.

My dear Friends, dwell in the life and power and love of God, and one towards another.

Friends, dwell in the measure of the spirit of God, and take heed to it, that you may grow in it—for the true and lasting love proceeds from God, who is eternal. Abiding in the measure of life, you will have peace and love that never changes. [But] if you turn from [that] measure, iniquity gets up—and so the love waxes cold, and in that lodge the evil thoughts, jealousies, evil will and murmurings.

Wait in the light, which is of God, that you may all witness the son of God, and witness that which never withers. So you will see and feel God near.

(Epistle No 117, 1656, p. 93; Works 7/115. See also Epistle No 77)

All Friends and brethren everywhere, wait in the life and power of the Lord—and none walk from it—that you may be made manifest to the light of Christ in every one, that the fear and dread of the Lord may be in all your hearts, that nothing may reign but life itself. So, keep all your Meetings in every place, waiting in the light, which comes from Christ the savour of your souls. That his presence in the midst of you all may feel, who are gathered together in his name and power, in his light (which is his name)—and are turned from the world's gatherings....

Therefore all Friends, this is a charge to you ...—walk in the light, life, power and wisdom of God; that you may be manifested—that it may be your witness—to that of God in every man....

All wait in the light for the wisdom by which all things were made, with it to use the Lord's creatures to his glory ...—for which end they were created. With the wisdom by which they were made—in the image of God—you may be kept out of the misuse of them; [so] that you may come to see that the earth is the Lord's, and the fulness thereof, and the earth may come to yield her increase, and enjoy her sabbaths....

So being kept in the light ... you come to receive the wisdom by which all things were made, and with it to order and use them to the glory of God....

(Epistle No 33, 1653, p. 28; Works 7/39)

~~~

The light shines in the darkness

Fox is prepared to look squarely at the dark side of man's nature. Sometimes his words fall unacceptably on our ears; sometimes they serve to make a contrast, and thereby heighten, the brilliance of the light he sees.

In the following epistle (which is printed complete except for minor repetitions) he however brings us—while waiting in the light—to be prepared to come to some recognition of the dark side of ourselves. The ideas and phrases he uses are all from the Bible—even though they are amongst those we perhaps most prefer to skim over.

Concerning the light

(To be read amongst Friends)

All Friends everywhere, keep your Meetings in the light which comes from the lord Jesus Christ. So will you receive power from him, and have the refreshing springs of life opened in your souls, and be kept sensible of the tender mercies of the Lord.

Know one another in the life … and in the power which comes from the lord Jesus Christ—who is your light, who is your life. [So] that in the life you may all see Christ reign in you—[him] who is the truth, and [from whom] you have light.

Here the old serpent is chained and put into the bottomless pit, and Christ is known to reign and you to reign with him—heirs with him, joint-heirs, heirs with God.

Here is received and witnessed the dominion of the world that is without end, and the promise of life from the father of life to you—[you] who are turned to the Son, who is the way to the Father, who is the mediator between the Father and you.

All wait to receive the everlasting priest, the everlasting covenant of God—[the covenant] of light, life and peace. No sin, no darkness nor death comes in to this covenant, but the blessing of the only wise God—the father of life—is known here, where no earthly man can approach.

He that is of God knows God's truth. But he that is of the devil does his lusts—[the devil] who was a murderer from the beginning, in whom there is no truth, who did not abide in truth. So he it is that speaks a lie, speaks of himself—and not God's word—for he is out of the truth.

But you, who are turned to the light, walk in the light, walk in the truth—where no darkness is. With [that] light—that never changes—you may come to see that which was in the beginning, before the world was, where there is no shadow or darkness.

As you wait in that light you will come to receive into your hearts the word of faith, which reconciles to God. [It] is as a hammer, to beat down all that is contrary; and as a sword, to divide the precious from the vile; and as a fire, to burn up that which is contrary to the precious.

[But that] word is pure and endures for ever; [it] was in the beginning, and is now witnessed and made manifest. Therefore wait in the light, that you all may receive it—

the same word that ever was, [and] from which the scriptures were given forth.

So, Friends, keep your Meetings. As you are moved of the Lord, be obedient to him, and keep your habitations. Be not troubled, but look to that which gives you [power] to see over the world.

So the lord God almighty preserve you all to his glory—Amen.

(Epistle No 105, 1655, p. 86; Works 7/107)

Fox knew what it meant to live in darkness—"Temptations grew more and more and I was tempted almost to despair ... I was under great misery and trouble ... I was a man of sorrows in the times of the first workings of the Lord in me." (Journal pp. 1–11)

Fox uses the word "temptation"; for Pilgrim it was the slough of despond; for Jesus it was forty days in the wilderness, tempted by the devil; for modern man it may be lostness, to be alone, depression, to despair.

Nowhere in his teaching does Fox direct us to the cloisters, to a monastery or nunnery, to the priest or doctor, to the confessional, to philosophy, theology or other worlds of the intellect. Where does he lead us to—but to the meeting for worship?

My dear Friends—Dwell in the power of the everlasting God, which [overcomes] the power of darkness and all the temptations in it. That will keep and bring you to the word which was in the beginning;

that will keep you up to the life, to feed upon the [life], [which is] over the power of darkness.

In that you will find strength, and feel dominion and life. That will let you see before the tempter was, and [see] over him. Into that the tempter cannot come, for he is out of the power and truth.

Dwell in that life, in which you will know dominion. Therefore let your faith be in the power, and over the weakness and temptations. Look not out at them, but look in the light and power of God at the Lord's strength, which will be made perfect in your weakest state.

Look at the grace of God in all temptations, to bring your salvation; this is your teacher to teach you—for when you look or hearken to the temptations you go from the teacher, the grace of God, and so are darkened.

The grace of God is sufficient, in all temptations, to lead out of them, and [sufficient] to keep over them.

(Epistle No 107, 1655, p. 87; Works 7/108)

The spiritual contribution
of women

On a number of occasions Fox wrote to Friends to urge the men to accept women as equals in the work of the church, and to encourage the women to play their full part. Mostly this relates to the women being help-meets to the men, or to take the prime responsibility in practical matters such as caring for the children or the unwell. All this might be expected. However, in the following text he is finding the basis for an equality at the deeper level of contributions made to the spiritual life of the gathered community.

Thus the interest for us is widened to include what Fox calls "prophecy"—for he applies this to men as to women.

The word "prophecy" is important in Fox's vocabulary. It goes with its fellows prophetic, to prophesy and a prophecy. A prophecy is usually a foretelling of something in the future, as we use to word. But the others have a considerably extended meaning for Fox. This is derived from his understanding of the purpose and role of the great prophets of the old testament, who were sent—virtually as God's messengers—to give greater awareness of God's truths for man.

Fox sees this work of awakening man's appreciation of spiritual truth as prophecy, one who does it is a prophet, and his or her teaching is prophetic.

The following quotations are from a pamphlet "The Woman Learning in Silence" published in 1656 (Smith's Cat. p. 651; Doctrinals p. 77; Works 4/104). Some importance must have been attached to it for it was republished with different beginning and ending five years later ("Concerning Sons and Daughters, and Prophetesses Speaking and Prophecying", 1661, Smith's Cat. p. 666). The full text has many of Fox's most tedious characteristics—verbose, repetitive, many digressions and, to us, an excessive reliance on biblical examples. Therefore parts have been paraphrased, to leave just the main theme.

Fox begins with a summary of Paul's views on women being silent in church, being subordinate, and learning from their husbands at home. This is from the law of the Hebrew church. But, says Fox:

Christ is one in the male and the female, [and he] makes free from the law. And the Lord days "I will pour out my spirit on all flesh, your sons and your daughters shall prophesy; your old men shall dream dreams and your young men shall see visions. Even upon your menservants and maid servants in those days I will pour out my spirit"....

Fox goes on to recall how Peter says "Paul wrote to you according to the wisdom given him, ... in all his letters. There

111

are some things in them hard to understand, which the ignorant and unstable twist to their own destruction."

You therefore, beloved, seeing you know these things, beware lest you also be led away with the error of the wicked, and fall from your own steadfastness; but grow in grace and the knowledge of our lord Jesus Christ, ...

Peter who was unlearned in the letter, but learned of Christ, says the scribes, pharisees, great rabbis and doctors, being not learned of Christ, knew not the scriptures.... Peter was learned in, knew and preached Christ, who was the life of the prophets and the end of the law.... So here the unlearned who was of the life, confounded all the learned [who were] out of the life....

Fox again summarizes Paul's words that husbands should love their wives and be not bitter against them; the husband is head of the wife as Christ is the head of the church, and saviour of the body; that as Christ loved the church and gave himself up for her, so husbands should love their wives as their own bodies.

"... and they twain shall be one flesh. This is a great mystery, I speak concerning Christ and the church." He that has an ear let him hear this great mystery. [But] the unlearned men wrest *[i.e. twist, distort]* it ... [they] know not this great mystery, ... [nor] the voice of his prophets, [and] are wondering at the prophesying of the daughters, ... the Lord's prophets....

As Joel, the Lord's prophet proclaimed that the Lord would pour out his spirit on all flesh:

Here all may see the spirit of the Lord not limited, ... and many thousands of servants and handmaids witness the spirit of the Lord poured out upon them, and the word of the Lord fulfilled. Upon the sons and daughters will the Lord pour out his spirit, and they shall prophesy. Many daughters and sons and young men and old men witness ... that visions are seen, old men dream dreams, and young men see visions and their sons and daughters do prophesy.

Fox recalls that at Pentecost, when the holy spirit fell upon the disciples, it was Joel's prophecy that was seen to be fulfilled; that Paul says "despise not prophesying"; that the Lord cautions "do my prophets no harm"; that Paul instructs how when two or three prophets speak in church the others should weigh what is said, thereby all may learn and all be encouraged; and how Moses said:

"Would God that all the Lord's people were prophets, and that the Lord would put his spirit upon them." Now mark Moses' answer, how backward Moses was from limiting the spirit, ...

And Anna the prophetess ... who served God with fasting and prayer night and day, came into the temple [and] spake of Christ to all those who looked for redemption in Jerusalem. Here was a large testimony borne of Jesus by Anna the prophetess—here you may see a daughter who gave testimony of Jesus. [It] would be, and still is a wonder in this our age, to see a woman of fourscore years of age to speak of Jesus ... as she did.

Fox tells of Priscella and Aquila, Phoebe and Mary who had helped Paul. And how...

Mary Magdelene came and told the disciples she had seen the Lord.... Here all may see it was Mary Magdelene who was sent to declare his resurrection.... Now you who make a scoff and a wonder at a woman's declaring, you may see it was Mary who first declared Christ after he was risen. So be ashamed and confounded for ever, and let all your mouths be stopped for ever—who despise the spirit of prophecy in daughters....

The apostle says "Christ in the male and in the female," and if Christ be in the female as well as in the male, is not he the same? May not the spirit of Christ speak in the female as well as in the male? Is he there to be limited? Who is there who dare limit the holy one of Israel? ... Who is it that dares stop Christ's mouth? ... For in that male where Christ reigns, rules and speaks, he will own Christ in the female, there to reign, rule and speak.... Christ is come to reign ... who now reigns in his sons and daughters ... that the glory is seen which the son had with his Father ... which glory these males and females who receive Christ do see....

Now every one having a light from Christ Jesus, ... see him, the prophet who God has raised up, which Moses spoke of, [he] who is the end of the prophets. With the light [they] see Christ... and receive him.... With the light you will see the promise to them of life, ... and everyone receiving the light which comes from Christ shall receive the spirit of prophecy—whether they be male or female.

The spirit of prophecy is the testimony of Jesus. If male and female have received the testimony of Jesus, they have received the spirit of prophecy.

Things may go wrong

Sometimes things go wrong, not only in the meeting for worship but also among the sharing fellowship. Fox had such situations to deal with, and he was outspoken in facing them. What may be more important, however, is how he went about it. Partly he always counter-balanced his criticism with a positive encouragement, partly it may be something in his approach.

Dearly beloved friends and brethren ... You must do nothing for the Lord by earthly policy, nor trust to that. But wait in the power of the lord God, and be ordered by that to his glory. You will never be right till then, and that must keep peace among you.

Take heed of highmindedness, for that will puff up that part which should not be exalted. If that [should] come up to rule [whatever] is for judgement, then it will do hurt. But when he whose right it is comes to reign, then peace and goodwill are to all men. And no hurt is seen in the holy mountain.

(Epistle No 75, 1654, p. 67; Works 7/85)

To Friends, concerning judging

Friends, to you all this is the word of the Lord: take heed of judging one another.... Neither lay open one another's weaknesses behind one another's backs....

But every one of you see yourselves in particular with the light of Christ ... that self may be judged out with the light.... Here all are in unity, here no self-will can arise, nor no mastery—but all that is judged out.

Let there be no back-biting amongst you, but speak to the others in love ...

And take heed ... of a feigned humility, and a feigned love—which is out of the light—and then to use that as a customary salutation or a formal gesture ...

So see that all your [actions] be in and from the light—here you will be kept clean and pure....

(Small part of Epistle No 48, 1653, p. 47; Works 7/61)

Concerning judging in meetings

Friends, do not judge one another in meetings—you who minister in the meetings. For your doing so has hurt people, both within and without, and you have brought yourselves under their judgement.

And you judging one another in the meetings has emboldened others to quarrel, and judge you also in the meetings. This has been out of order, and [out] of the church order also.

Now, if you have anything to say to any, stay till the meeting be done, and then speak to them in private between yourselves, and do not lay open one another's weakness—for that is weakness and not wisdom to do so.

For your judging one another in meetings has almost destroyed some Friends, and distracted them.

This is for want of love which bears all things—and therefore let it be amended.

No more, but my love....

(Epistle No 173, 1659, p. 135; Works 7/166)

All Friends, take heed of running on in a form, lest you lose the power. But keep in the power and seed of God, in which you will live in the substance.

At any disputes take heed. Many may be lifted up in the victory and conquest, and have a joy in the prophecies and openings, [but] after fall.

If babblers come and janglers [argue], they have a bad meeting. So the murmuring nature gets up, out of patience and the seed—which bears all things and suffers all things. [Patience] keeps down that which causes lifting up, murmuring and disputing.

But the seed and prophecy ends [that], and keeps down all which is contrary.... That which keeps down [changeable things] is the peace, the corner-stone, and the stayedness in the seed and life.

(Epistle No 116, 1656, p. 92; Works 7/114)

Fox had occasion to reprimand Friends somewhere for sleeping in meeting for worship. Of course it was more difficult for them. Quakers and everyone else in their churches usually had at least two hours' worship on Sunday morning, then a lunch break, then two more hours in the afternoon. A religious meeting might even run for three hours.

If we had to tackle a difficult situation, we might not use such stern words. But what could we do for the positive guidance that embraces the rebuke?

Dear Friends—Be faithful in the service of God, and mind the Lord's business, and be diligent. So will the power of the Lord be brought over those who have gainsayed it....

Friends, all take heed of sleeping in meetings, and sottishness and dulness. For it is an unsavoury thing to see one sit nodding in a meeting and so to lose the sense of the Lord.

It is both a shame and a sadness, and it grieves the upright and watchful *[this then also meant waking]* who wait upon the Lord, to see such things.

It is a shame and an unseemly thing for the priests, people and others who come in to your meetings—and see you who come together to worship God, to meet together to wait upon him, and to have fellowship in his spirit—for you to sit nodding.

Therefore be careful and watchful—and let it be mended.

Mind the light and power of Christ Jesus in you. That will condemn all such things, and lead you out of and above such things; and make you watchful over one another for your good.

(Epistle No 257, 1668, p. 257; Works 7/308)

George Fox on ministry
in meeting

Fox did not write much about ministry and vocal prayer in meeting for worship—he was more concerned to assert the potentiality of worshipping in silence, at a time when hour-long sermons were the norm. Most of what he had to say about ministry was directed to those who spoke to others outside the Quaker community. However, while having been careful to avoid taking his words out of context, we can see from the following extracts what he felt to be the centre from which true ministry springs, and the source or quality that allows it to carry conviction and makes the heart to respond.

First, a tiny scrap—

So if any have any thing upon them to speak, in the life of God stand up and speak it—if it be but two or three words—and sit down again. And keep in the life, that you may answer that of God in every man upon the earth....

(From Epistle No 150, 1657, p. 116 ; Works 7/143)

To Friends in the ministry—Stand up, you prophets of the Lord, for the truth upon the earth. Quench not your prophecy, neither heed them who despise you, but stand in that which brings you through to the end.

Heed not the eyes of the world, ... but answer that in them all, which they have closed their eye to; so you may tell them of things to come, answering that of God in them that shall remain....

And you daughters, to whom it is given to prophesy, keep within your own measure, seeing over that which is without, answering that of God in all.

Despise not the prophecy, keep down that nature which would [despise it]....

Neither be lifted up in your openings and prophecies, lest you depart from that which opened, and so come to be judged by the son of God, and be bidden to depart as workers of iniquity ...

Quench not the spirit.... For if the spirit be quenched ... evil is put for good and good for evil; ... then you cannot try all things ... [nor] hold fast to that which is good, ... [nor] see good. But when the spirit is not quenched, then with the spirit you may see the good—to take the good and to shun the evil. This brings to put a difference between the precious and the vile, the profane and the holy, the clean and the unclean. The spirit that is in you proves all things.

(Epistle No 35, 1653, p. 31; Works 7/43)

So all who feel the power stirring in them to minister, when they have done let them live in the power and in the truth and in the grace which keeps in the seasoned words, and which keeps a stabilized and seasoned life.

So all may minister as they have received the grace. So every one is a steward of the grace of God—if he does not turn the grace of God into wantonness. And so to minister in that love and grace and power which keeps all things in subjection and order, and [keeps] in unity in the life and in the power and light, by which you may see that of God in every man, and answer to that which God has showed unto his people.

For the true labourers in the vineyard do answer that of God, the true ministers bring people to that which is to instruct them—viz. the spirit of God. So [they] are ministers of the spirit, and ministers of the grace. They answer the spirit and the grace and truth in all, in which all that do minister have unity, and through which they have fellowship with God and Christ.

(Epistle No 267, 1669, p. 300; Works 8/13)

The following extracts are from an epistle when Fox encourages Friends whose ministry is subject to criticism by worldly people. He often contrasts ministry "in the spirit" with that derived from book-learning,

In the full epistle he refers to Joel's prophecy that "sons and daughters shall prophesy", and adds biblical illustrations of the wells and springs of living water, and of the glistering or glistening pearl that is beyond all price—all manifestations of the spirit.

Then we see how he expands the Biblical imagery, and links it to a theme that he often uses—that the disciples and apostles were just ordinary men, drawn from everyday trades and occupations.

All Friends everywhere dwell in the living spirit and power and in the heavenly light. Quench not the motions of it in yourselves, nor the movings of it in others.... Therefore be obedient to the power of the Lord, and his spirit, and his spiritual weapons; war with that philistine who would stop up your wells and springs. Jacob's well was in the mountains ... and belief in the power keeps the spring open ... that everyone's cup may run over. For you may all prophesy one by one, and the spirit of the prophets is subject to the prophets.... So in the light everyone should have something to offer, and to offer an offering in righteousness to the living God....

Now Friends, if [Joel's prophecy] be fulfilled ... everyone [is] to feel the spirit of God, by which you may see the things of God and declare them to his praise. For with the heart man believes, and with the mouth confession is made unto salvation. First, he has it in his heart, before it comes out of his mouth; and this is beyond that brain-beaten-heady stuff which man has long studied....

So with the holy ghost and with the light and power of God, do you build upon Christ the foundation and life. By the same heavenly light and power and spirit do you labour in the vineyard, and do you minister and speak forth the things of God, and do you dig for the pearls. Therefore bring them forth, and let them be seen how they glister—the glistering pearls. All come into the heavenly vineyard of God to labour ... that every one of you may have your penny, that precious penny, and heavenly treasure from God almighty....

Friends, you see how men and women can speak enough for the world, for merchandise, for husbandry, the plowman for his plow; but when they should come to speak for God, they quench the spirit ... and do not obey God's will.

But come, let us see what the wise merchants can say. Have they found the pearl and field, and purchased the field which yield these glorious glistering pearls? Let us see what you can say for God and that heavenly merchandise. What can the plowmen say for God with his spiritual plow? Is the fallow ground plowed up? Has he abundance of the heavenly seed of life? So what can the heavenly husbandman say, has he abundance of heavenly fruit in store? What can the thresher say, has he gotten the wheat out of the sheaf, the heavenly wheat, with his heavenly flail? And let us see, what can the heavenly plowman, husbandman and thresher say for God? How have they laboured in the vineyard that they may have their penny? Some are breakers of clods in the vineyard; some are weeders; some are cutting off the branches and bushes, and fitting *[making fit]* the ground, and cutting up the roots with the heavenly axe for the seed; some are harrowing in; some are gathering and laying up the riches. So you may see, here are merchants, plowmen, harrowers, weeders, reapers, threshers in God's vineyard; yet none are to find fault one with another, but every one labouring in their places, praising the Lord, looking to him for their wages, their heavenly penny of life from the Lord of life....

Come, fishermen, what have you caught with your nets? What can you say for God? Your brethren, Peter and John, fishermen, could say much for God. Read in the Acts and you may see it. I would not have you degenerate from their spirit.

Shepherds and herdsmen, where are you? What can you say now for God, whose abiding is much in the fields? David, Jacob and Amos, your fellow shepherds and herdsmen (do you not see?)—they could say much for God. I would have you to be like them, and not degenerate from their spirit.

Come tradesmen, tent-makers, physicians and custom-men, what can you say for God? Do you not read that your fellow tradesmen in ages past could say much for God? Do not degenerate from their spirit. Do you not remember the accusations of the wise and learned Grecians, when the apostle preached Christ among them, that they were called poor tradesmen and fishermen? Therefore be faithful. The preachers of Jesus Christ now are the same to the wise of the world as then.

(Epistle No 275, 1669, p. 305; Works 8/19)

Fox saw that preaching, ministry and prayer may take many different forms, including giving praise and thankfulness in

joyousness. The following passages express this, and are the more remarkable in that he wrote this epistle when imprisoned—at Worcester, an imprisonment that excessively sapped his health and strength.

He again speaks of singing, and while we might today find this perhaps disturbing in meeting for worship, at least we might sing in our hearts.

All Friends that are in the power of God and in his spirit—Through this spirit you pray unto God, and ask in the name of Christ Jesus (which all true prayers are to be in). And the true singing and rejoicing are to be in the spirit, and the true preaching and ministry are to be in the spirit. For the saints made able ministers of the spirit, and not of the letter.

Now when a minister, in the spirit of the living God, does minister spiritual and heavenly things, they who receive them with joy in the assembly, ... [they] receive them in sincerity, with joy and gladness, and rejoice in the receiving of them, ...

And likewise they that do sing in the spirit do reach to the spirit in others, whereby they have a sense that it proceeds from the spirit. For at the hearing of the speech of the true minister, there is joy to all who thirst and seek after righteousness. For the preaching of the gospel is glad-tidings, the joyful news, and is a comfort both to soul, body and spirit—to all who receive it in integrity and sincerity. They cannot but rejoice at the sound of the power, where it is received....

Oh! the everlasting gospel, the everlasting power of God—which is liberty where this is heard (the sound of it), [this] is the liberty of the spirit, to the soul, to the creature. If a creature should praise God in his soul, in his spirit, in the very hearing of the sound of this glorious gospel, or make a joyful melody....

(*Epistle No 312, 1674, p. 344; Works 8/64*)

Cautions on ministry
from the wrong centre

From the earliest days Fox saw the possibility of ministry from the wrong centre. Sometimes he spoke out against it directly, sometimes he sought to show why it is inadequate to its true purpose.

Friends, I do warn you in the presence of the living God, not to speak of things of God out of [*away from*] the fear of God, at random, in a presumptuous mind. For proud boasters are excluded from the kingdom of God, and condemned with the light of Christ; and they are judged with the life which gave forth the scriptures.

Therefore ... wait in the light and love it. It will bring you to stand in the counsel of God, and keep you from all wicked ways. With it you will see all the enchanters—false prophets—who speak a divination from their own brain....

(*Epistle No 34, 1653, p. 30; Works 7/41*)

~~~

Let no Friend go beyond their own measure given them of God, nor rejoice in another man's line made ready to their hands—lest they get up and would be justified which is to be condemned. That which will boast, and be justified in the sight of men, is excluded out of the kingdom.

Therefore wait in the measure of life, and with it be led to have power over your own wills (which are mortal and changeable), that the way of righteousness may be found. [It is in that way] where your wills are shut out—which cause hastiness and strife, and cause to run into words without the life—[and] where judgement and condemnation do overtake you.

Wherefore delight in judgement, which leads to the door of mercy.

(Epistle No 118, 1656, p. 93; Works 7/115)

~~~

To Friends, concerning openings, etc.

This is the word of the Lord to you all. In all openings and speakings let not the man be lifted up—for that will not be the servant but the master. [That] is to be thrown down from that whence the openings come. Therefore keep down that which would be lifted up in the sight of the world, for that (often) falls in the sight of the world. But that being lifted up which answers that of God in every man, this is of the son of

God—who is exalted above the world, and was before it was made and exalted.

Every one dwell in the seed and life of God, and in that know one another. And meet together and keep your Meetings, that you may see the lord Jesus Christ in the midst of you.

(Epistle No 152, 1657, p. 117; Works 7/144)

Section Four

Major insights of George Fox

George Fox on the offices of Christ

*In his teaching Fox laid great emphasis on the offices of Christ;
is was one of the formative concepts that gave structure and
cohesion to much that he taught, throughout his ministry.*

*Fox uses the word "offices" in our ordinary way where an
officer occupies a post and functions appropriately. He allies it
to his concept that Christ is alive and present, and may be
experienced directly. Thus this spiritual entity may be experienced in many different functional roles, to which we can
respond or react—so that it means something, so that something happens to us.*

*Two points should be added. When Fox spells this out, he
uses a phrase like "Christ may be known as he is in his office of
king." He does not say Christ **is** a king, but that he functions at
that moment as if he were a king. Secondly, although Fox
teaches of many offices, Christ does not exist nor is experienced*

in of all those roles at the same instant—but just the one to suit your need.

In the following text Fox spells out this teaching fully; almost certainly he is recalling his ministry or a proclamation somewhere. Although he left a note that it should be published, it never has been. Small wonder that we do not own him as a spiritual giant. Manuscript 53E Aa bound with the Annual Catalogue, edited by Joseph Pickvance and Hugh Ross.

Now Friends, you know that the priests used to catechize you and asked "How many offices Christ had in his church?" And they put down in their catechism "There are three". So, you that are catechized, when they ask you that question, you say "Three; Christ had three offices". Then they will ask you what they are, and you will tell him, as it is said in the catechism "His priestly office, his prophetic office and his kingly office". Then the priest will say "Well said, old man, lass or lad. You have spoken very well". So you and they think it is a great matter to say those words.

But do you think Christ has no more offices in his church than these three—Christ's priestly office, and prophetic office, and kingly office? We who believe in the light which Christ has commanded us to believe in, we believe there are more, and that we shall find more in the scriptures of truth.

But, first, as to those three offices, I shall speak something. First, his prophetic office, that is, his office as Christ is a prophet.

It is the work of a prophet to open spiritual truths to people; to show them things to come; to show them the joy and the judgement; the comfort and the sorrow; the ways of the Lord and the ways of the wicked; and that which they should walk in and that which they should not.

So Christ is a prophet—this great prophet that is raised up by the Lord; who in the midst of his church opens to his people—by his power and his spirit and by his light—opens to them things to come, and shows them the way of salvation, and shows them the ways of destruction, and the way of life and the way of death.

So, where two or three are gathered in his name, there he is in the midst of them, exercising his prophetic office by his power and by his spirit. People who believe in the light, as Christ has commanded them, hear him, their prophet, speaking unto them, showing them the life and the glory that is of the Father and of himself.

Secondly, Christ exercises the office of a priest. Where does he exercise this office, but in the midst of his people?—where two or three are gathered together in his name.

Is it the work of the priests to sacrifice and to offer offerings, first for their own sins and then for the people's. But Christ offers up himself. Therefore feel Christ the priest in the midst of you, sanctifying you and cleansing you and purifying you and making you clean—that he might present you perfect to God.

So know Christ exercising his priestly office by his power and spirit, for you to be made alive by him, and gathered in his name.

Thirdly, Christ exercises the office of a king. Now, it is the office of a king to rule, to give forth laws, and to reign. Christ reigns by his power and his spirit in the hearts of his people, and he subdues his enemies, the devil and his works. He brings all to be subject to him— as they have been subject to the prince of darkness and death. So Christ gives forth his law of life to his subjects, his law of love, his law of faith, his law of his spirit. He exercises his ruling power and light and life in the midst of his church.

Now we will see what offices Christ Jesus has besides these three of prophet, priest and king. We shall see if we can find any more in the scripture than the priests have put in their catechism.

Is not Christ called a bishop? Has he not the office of a bishop? Is it not to oversee? Is not Christ called the bishop of the soul, to oversee the soul, and oversee the mind and the spirit when they go astray? So where two or three are gathered in his name Christ is in the midst of them, in their hearts, as he is a bishop. In overseeing them he is the anchor of the soul, an anchor to stay the ship in times of waves and storms, who stays the soul which is immortal up to God who is immortal.

Is not Christ said to be minister of the sanctuary and true tabernacle, that God has pitched? So where two or three are gathered he is in the midst of them as a minister, to minister grace and eternal things, to minister faith and light and life and peace to them. Is not this an office, a minister? This makes five.

Is not Christ said to be a shepherd? Is that not an office, to look after his sheep? It is the office of an outward shepherd to look to the outward sheep, and help them out of the briars and brambles, to help them out of the pit and ponds; to feed them in pastures, and drive them to the spring and brooks to drink.

So Christ is a shepherd in the midst of his people who are gathered in his name. He exercises the office of a shepherd in the midst of them, in their hearts. When their minds go astray, he plucks them back again with his heavenly crook, and so keeps the soul and mind from the dogs, wolves, ravening beasts and devouring fowls. He keeps the soul and spirit upon the pastures of life, and the springs of life—Oh! blessed shepherd for ever!

Christ is a physician, that's an office is it not? Where two or three are gathered in his name he is in the midst of them to heal them, to anoint them with the oil of gladness, to cure them of all their diseases and wounds, to bind up the broken hearted, to anoint their eyes and unstop their ears—that they may see and hear the prophet, and make them perfectly whole. This makes seven offices.

Christ is a preacher. God has anointed him to preach. Is that not an office? That makes eight. So where two or three are gathered in his name is not he in the midst of them as a preacher? He preaches to them the way of life and salvation, he preaches heavenly things.

Again, Christ is said to be a counsellor. Is he not in the midst of his people as he is a counsellor?—counselling them the way of salvation, redemption and righteousness, holiness and truth, which is the way of life.

For if people should lose their outward estate, and their landmarks of their outward inheritance, do not they run to an outward counsellor; he looks in the books and records and they receive counsel, their landmarks are shown to them, and their minds are quieted.

So God has given Christ as a counsellor—he has all the books and records in his hand, and therefore all people must go to him. "But which way?" cry they. The way of the just is a shining light. Christ has enlightened you, that with the light you may see him; he bids you believe in it, that you may walk in the paths of the just. So come to him your counsellor—he will show you where your landmark is, and by his power throw off the rubbish that the man of sin has thrown on your landmark. So, the rubbish being thrown off in you, then you will see your landmark, the landmark of salvation—and you will see an inheritance of a life and a kingdom, an inheritance that has no end. Then there's joy in the inward man.

Tenthly, Christ is said to be a captain. Where two or three are gathered in Christ's name he is a captain exercising his office. He exercises, he trains, he disciplines his soldiers with the heavenly armour of light, the shield of faith, breastplate of righteousness, the helmet of salvation, the sword of the spirit which is the word of God, and their feet are shod with the preparation of the gospel of peace. This armour of righteousness and light glistens upon Christ's soldiers. Christ disciplines them to march and not to draw back, but to go on against the man of sin.

So if you have this armour of light and the word of God, Christ your captain will order you with his iron rod, that you may know how to handle your arms—that you may resist the devil though he may go like a roaring lion seeking whom he may devour. You will be such as the apostles were, they knew how to handle their arms, who resisted the devil and stood steadfast in the faith.

Further, the scripture says God has given him for a mediator, interceder and leader. Do not the priests say that the Quakers deny Christ's office as a mediator? But if the office of Christ be a mediator, this makes eleven offices....

(The rest of that manuscript is missing. These pages are condensed somewhat from the original.)

There follow four texts that are typical of the way in which Fox uses his teaching on the offices of Christ.

To have your rest in Christ

From an epistle from George Fox to Friends in a time of trouble.

And now the Lord has sought and searched and found and gathered you, to feed you atop of the mountains with his heavenly bread, and set one shepherd over you—the shepherd over all the living that are made alive by him. So the Lord has the glory of seeking and gathering out of the wilderness, pits, groves and ditches of old Adam and the serpent, with his brambles and briars.

So Christ is the rest[ing place] of the living that he has made alive, and is the shepherd to feed them with life and the springs of life. [He] is the bishop of their souls, who oversees them so that they do not go out of the pastures of life and from the springs of life or the fold of life.

It is a glorious pasture—to be fed atop of all the mountains, in the life, in the pastures of life, with the living shepherd. And to be overseen by the living bishop, and to be sanctified, and to be presented to God by the living priest, and to be counselled by the living counsellor of everlasting salvation, and to be of a kingdom and of a world and an inheritance that has no end.

And now that you have an everlasting preacher whom God has appointed to preach, and an everlasting minister who ministers grace and life and salvation and truth to you, [and] an everlasting prophet that God has raised up who is to be heard—all the living hear him— so none can silence, stop the mouth, or take away your shepherd, your bishop, your minister, your preacher, your prophet, your counsellor. So in Christ, the heavenly man, you have rest.

I say sit down in Christ, who was before the world was, for all wearisomeness is out of him, but in him you have rest.

(From a General Epistle to Friends, presumed date 1670. Epistles No 279 p. 311; Works 8/25)

Why shall we not sit in silence?

No doubt this was another great proclamation.

There is a cry in the world among professors and papists and protestants against our silent meetings. For when Friends are met together waiting upon the Lord and Jesus Christ their teacher, some priests and professors have come and looked upon us in our meetings. The priests have said "Did you ever see the like in your lives? Look how they sit mumming and dumbing here, what edification is there among them?" "I never see the like in my life" cry the rest of the priests and professors—"Come let us go away, here is no edification, here are no words. See how they sit mumming and dumbing!"

So when they are gone away, it may be some Friends have been moved of the Lord to say to them "Did you never see the like in your life, nor never in your days?" Say they to them "Prithee, look into your own steeple-houses, yes in all the steeple-houses among papists and protestants, and see—do not your people sit mumming and dumbing under you?" And have you not got a law that if anyone ask you a question when you are speaking or afterwards, do you not cry "Where are the churchwardens or constables? Is there not an officer here? Take him away, for he has disturbed me!" So do you not keep them in this manner, mumming and dumbing till they be three score years of age—all their life time?

There is not so much liberty to ask a question although your doctrine be never so false. So you may do what you will without questioning of it.

So look into your own parish. Did you never see the like in your life? You may see it all over christendom—all people sit mumming and dumbing under you. Every one has got a law; how many have you persecuted for questioning of you? So you keep the people in the mumming and dumbing state.

Why shall we not sit under our minister Christ Jesus, and our preacher Christ Jesus whom God has raised to preach?—as your people sit under your preachers who you have made at schools by men, and have opened your mouths and men may stop you.

Why shall we not sit under our bishop Christ Jesus, who is our overseer?—as you sit under your bishop that you have made.

Why shall we not sit under our shepherd Christ Jesus who gives us life, yea abundantly, we know his voice?—and we know the hireling who will fly when the wolf comes.

Why shall we not sit under our prophet whom God and not man has raised up, whom he commands us to hear? He who will not hear him must be cut off. Our prophet is like unto Moses, and is to be heard in all things. Moses commands us to hear him, God commands to hear Christ Jesus, Christ commands to hear him. "Learn of me" says Christ, "This is my beloved son, hear him" says God.

What if we be sitting under our prophet and bishop and preacher etc, and hear him? Hear what he says to our souls? David said he would hear what God said to his soul—that is by hearing what Christ says. And God must have our ears to hear and to hearken to him.

But you ministers made of men "never see the like". It's likely you never did! You never heard God's voice, nor Christ's, but run when God never sent you. Yet you will tell us "Christ will be with you to the end of the world"—and yet you never heard his voice. You will be found with a lie in your mouth—"he be with you to the end of the world" and he never spoke to you!

Why shall we not sit under our counsellor Christ Jesus? He whom God has given us for a counsellor to lead us out of the world to the ways of salvation, to a kingdom and a world that has no end.

Why shall we not sit under our leader Christ Jesus who leads to the image of God, and holiness and righteousness?—we who have forsaken the blind leaders that lead us into the ditch....

(From manuscript 82E Aa bound with Annual Catalogue, never before published.)

An incident with the constables

On some occasions Fox placed the offices of Christ at the centre of what he had to say. The following incident, taken from his Journal (but not included in Nickall's version), is an example. It arose in London, at a time of political unrest; the authorities, acting on the word of informers, sent constables to prevent any gathering or meeting, lest it be used to plan insurrection. Sometimes soldiery were used to break up meetings. Ordinary church services were exempt, but malicious people easily brought the anxious magistrates to foreclose Quaker meetings of worship.

One first-day it was upon me to go to Devonshire House meeting in the afternoon; and because I had heard friends were kept out [of] there in the morning (as they were that day at most meetings about the city), I went somewhat the sooner, and got into the yard before the soldiers came to guard the passages; but the constables were got there before me, and stood in the door-way with their staves. I asked them to let me go in; they said "they could not, nor durst not; for they were commanded the contrary, and were sorry for it". I told them I would not press upon them; so I stood by, and then one gave me a stool to sit down on.

After a while the power of the Lord began to spring up among Friends, and one began to speak. The constable soon forbade him, and said he should not speak; and he not stopping they began to be wroth. But I gently laid my hand upon one of the constables, and wished him to let him alone; the constable did so, and was quiet; and the man did not speak for long.

After he had done, I was moved to stand up and speak. In my declaration I said "They need not come against us with swords and staves, for we were a peaceable people; and had nothing in our hearts but goodwill to the king and magistrates, and to all people upon the earth. We did not meet, under pretence of religion, to plot and contrive against the government, or to raise insurrections; but to worship God in spirit and in truth. We had Christ to be our bishop, priest, and shepherd to feed us and oversee us, and he ruled in our hearts; so we could all sit in silence, enjoying the teacher. So to Christ, their bishop and shepherd I recommended them all".

I then sat down. After a while I was moved to pray, and the power of the Lord was over all; and the people, the constables, the soldiers put off their hats. When the meeting was done, and Friends began to pass away, the constable put off his hat, and desired the Lord to bless us; for the power of the Lord was over him and the people, and kept them under.

(1683, Ellwood's Journal p. 502; Works 2/255)

You know...

Towards the end of his life, Fox wrote to Friends in Wales giving thanks for messages received, telling that the Quaker faith prospered in England, and giving encouragement and exhortation, part expressed within the offices of Christ.

Dear friends and brethren, in the lord Jesus Christ, whom he has gathered to himself by his glorious hand and power; who is the rock of ages and the foundation of many generations, that cannot be shaken; in which you all have life, peace, rest, salvation and eternal happiness....

Our desire is that you all may live and walk in Christ, and set[tle down] in him, in his grace and truth; and that you may answer the truth of God in all people with the word of life; and also answer the good in all, with a godly and a holy life and [behaviour]....

Now, all dear Friends, you know your teacher and leader Christ Jesus. And you know him your high priest who is made higher than the heavens by the power of an endless life; by whom you are made a royal priesthood, to offer up spiritual sacrifices to God by Jesus Christ. And you know there is no other way to God but by Jesus Christ. And you know God has raised him up a prophet in the new testament, who is to be heard in all things, who opens and no man can shut, and shuts and no man can open. And you know that Christ is the bishop of your souls, to oversee you [so] that you do not go astray from God. And you know that Christ is the true shepherd, and has laid down his life for his sheep; [he] is to be heard and followed, who gives unto his sheep life eternal.

So abide in him who is your life eternal and everlasting, in whom you have peace with the everlasting God. Amen.

(Epistle No 406, 1685, p. 541; Works 8/292)

George Fox on Christ the teacher

Now to turn to the second of these major insights.

Something happened during Fox's lifetime to turn 60,000 people to be Quakers. When Fox wanted to describe that "something" briefly, the phrase he used was "Christ has come to teach his people himself." What did he mean by Christ being a teacher?

In its simplest form he sees the spirit of Christ as a teacher of the truths of the scriptures, and the base for those who wrote them. Fox could see their relevance and the inter-relation of different passages, yet he always attributed this to the working of the spirit.

Secondly, we need to consider a practical situation. When Fox and the other ministers travelled around preaching their gospel, people were urged to meet together in silent worship, and were told that in the quiet they would find something. This they did, but they tended to find different things, and followed different paths. So within a few years Fox and the others went round these Meetings again, seeking to lead their members to the spiritual richness he had found, to bring them to a unity. This was called "settling" the Meetings. And the phrase Fox most often uses for this was "they were brought to Jesus Christ their teacher."

Third, Fox proclaimed Christ as the teacher of righteous-ness—learning of the right relationship between God and man, and then living it out in daily life. Fox constantly looked to Jesus, the prophets and the apostles and found there the clues to this right relationship. Through his spiritual sensitivity he experienced a power of God to bring this relationship to fruition, and to apply it to the affairs of daily life. This is what he proclaimed as being accessible to, and attainable by, others.

Fortunately we have a text by Fox in which he expounded his understanding of the role of Christ as a teacher, in what God and Christ teaches us, and what we might learn. It was directly mainly to people in other churches. In much shortened form (with added sub-headings) it follows.

Christ is come to teach his people himself

And the word of the Lord is to you, that God is come and is coming to teach his people himself, by his son Jesus Christ.

For the lord God made man and woman in his image and placed them in paradise; he was their teacher, guide and orderer, who taught them what to do and what to leave undone. As long as they kept under God's teaching they were happy, and kept in the image and likeness of God and in his righteousness and holiness, and in the paradise of God. But when they forsook God's teaching and hearkened to the serpent's teaching, they lost the likeness of God and were driven out of paradise, and so came into darkness, sin and misery.

Now Christ being come, he says "learn of me, I am the way, the truth and the life; and no man comes to the Father but by me." So here you may see Christ is the teacher again, who is the way to God.

To hear Christ

Moreover, God says "this is my beloved son, in whom I am well pleased, hear ye him." So here all people are to believe in and hear from the son and learn of him.

The apostle says to the Hebrews "God, who at sundry times and in divers manners, spoke in times past to the fathers by the prophets, has in these last days spoken to us by his son."

So here you may see that God, who was the first speaker in paradise to Adam and Eve, was the speaker again to the apostles and to the church in primitive times, by Christ Jesus.

So the same God, I say, is the same speaker in these days by Christ his son, to his people; and he renews us up in the image of God and righteousness and holiness, as they were in before they fell.

This is my message to you all—That God was the first teacher and speaker to Adam and Eve in paradise, and was the speaker and teacher to the apostles and church in primitive times, and is now come to teach his people himself by his son, if you will hear him.

God's spirit poured over all men

B ut now you may object, and say how shall we hear him? And where? And when?

The answer is—God poured out his spirit upon the house of Isreal, to whom he gave his law, that they might understand his law and hear his voice (Ezekeil 39:29).

And Moses said "Like unto me will God raise up a prophet, him shall you hear in all things." This prophet is Christ Jesus—as you may see in Acts 3:24 to the end.

And in Joel 2 and Acts 2 they said "How God would pour out his spirit on all flesh."

So now God pours out his spirit on all flesh. With and by this spirit all flesh may see the salvation of God, and all hear God and Christ, his son by whom God speaks.

The light reveals evil and grace redeems

A s John says "In the beginning was the word, in the word was life, and the life was the light of men"; and that "was the true light which lights every man that comes into the world"; and Christ says "Believe in the light, that you may become children of the light."

So by belief in the spiritual, heavenly and divine light, which is the life in Christ the word, they come to be grafted into Christ, the heavenly root bears them, and so become children of the light.

So here you may see Christ Jesus is the light which lets you see all your sins that you have acted or committed, and all your evil words or thoughts; and so this same light will also let you see your saviour Christ Jesus, from whence the light comes to save you from your sins.

For the apostle says "The grace of God that brings salvation has appeared to all men, teaching us that denying ungodliness and worldly lusts, we should live soberly and godly in this present world." (Titus 2:11–12)

Now this is all the true Christians' teacher, the grace of God which brings their salvation. So if all men have and know salvation, it is brought to them by this grace of God, their teacher.

Grace comes from the gospel

Now, should you enquire from whence comes this grace? The answer is—The law came by Moses to the house of Israel, upon whom God poured out his spirit that they might understand. But now this grace of God and truth comes by Jesus Christ, who has appeared to all men to teach them and bring them salvation.

Now, when Christ was with his disciples, he sent them first to preach salvation to the lost sheep of the house of Israel, and not to go into the way of the gentiles. After Christ was risen from the dead, he gave his disciples a larger commission, and bid them then "go into all nations, and preach the gospel to every creature under heaven."

So God poured out his spirit so that they might understand his gospel; and by his grace they might receive his gospel.

So this everlasting gospel being preached again, and received again, so the glorious fellowship of the gospel, and salvation is known again, and received and obeyed by us.

The worship in truth

So all people must come to the spirit, and know the spirit in their hearts, and the truth there, that they may worship and serve God in spirit and in truth. This is the worship that Christ set up above 1600 years ago. Now, in this, the standing, perfect and catholic worship in the spirit and the truth, must God the Father be worshipped.

This spirit of truth all true Christians witness; it proceeds from the Father and son; it leads us out of all error into all truth—all such are led and guided and taught by it, up to God from whence it comes.

Certain offices of Christ

How does Christ exercise his offices in you, and amongst you?

Does not the Lord say "that he has given Christ for a witness, a leader and commander to the people"? Now, is not he come? Is he your leader and commander? Examine yourselves. All that call yourselves Christians, are not you to follow his leading by his power, light and spirit, and grace, and gospel, and to obey his commands?

His office as he is a counsellor; do you hear his voice from heaven, concerning your heavenly state?

His office as he is a shepherd; are you his sheep, and do you hear his voice? Do you follow him, and do you know his voice? Does he lead you into his pastures of life?

Likewise, how does Christ exercise his office as he is a bishop to oversee you, with the heavenly spirit, light and grace, and as the head of his church?

How does Christ exercise his office as he is a priest amongst you? Do you feel his pure water washing you, that he may present you holy and without blemish to God?

How do you feel Christ exercising his office as a prophet amongst you? Do you hear him in all things? Does he reveal the Father to you? Does he open the book of conscience to you? And the book of the law, and the book of the prophets, and the book of parables, and the book of life? So that you may see Christ, who is the rock in this age to build upon, who is the foundation of the prophets and apostles, and your foundation now to build upon.

How does he exercise his kingly office amongst or in you? Does he rule in your hearts by faith? So Christ the heavenly and spiritual man is your ruler—by his power and faith and spirit and grace in your hearts.

The faith that works by love

Does not the apostle bid the church in his days, to "look unto Jesus the author and finisher of their faith"? Now, must people look anywhere else but to Jesus? Is not this the faith that they are to contend for? Is not this the one faith they have from the one Lord? And so are not all the true Christians to walk in the steps of this faith, which is the faith of Abraham and the gift of God?

Is not this the faith that works by love? Does not the apostle tell the church of the Corinthians that, if they had not love, all their prophesying and their speaking, though with the tongues of men and angels, yet if they had not charity (or love) it was but as sounding brass and tinkling cymbals.

The new covenant and its bounty

The Lord said to Jeremiah "Behold the days come, I will make a new covenant with the house of Israel, not according to the old. I will put the laws in their inward parts, and write them in their hearts; I will be their God, and they shall be my people."

So now all the Christians that profess the days of this new covenant, Christ Jesus—has God written his laws in your hearts, and put them in your inward parts and in your minds? Do you all know the Lord, by Christ Jesus the new covenant? Are you in this high and glorious and everlasting covenant? Can you say that God is your God, and you are his people?

And in Micah where the Lord says "many nations shall come and say—let us go up into the mountain of the Lord, and he shall teach us of his ways, and we will walk in his paths, and they shall sit every man under his vine and under his fig-tree, and none shall make them afraid." (4:1–4)

Now you may see, here are nations that will come under God's teaching, who teaches them this way and path to walk in. They that are under God's teaching sit under Christ the vine, and are grafted into him, and they that abide in him will bring forth fruit.

The invitation

The prophet said "Like unto me will God raise up a prophet, him you shall hear in all things"; so here you are all invited to hear the son. And when the son of God was come into the world, he said "whosoever believes in me, he shall not perish but have everlasting life." And God said "this is my beloved son, in whom I am well pleased, hear ye him."

And Christ says "learn of me", and tells you "he is the way, the truth and the life, and no-one comes to the Father but by him"; he invites you also to come. He says to all the weary and heavy laden, he calls them to come to him, for his burden is light and his yoke is easy, that they might find rest for their souls. The apostle invites you to come unto Christ, and bids you "look unto him who is the author and finisher of your faith."

Christ tells you "that all power in heaven and earth is given unto him" and every creature is to have a visitation of his gospel. Therefore he sent his disciples unto every nation to preach it; he enlightens all with his heavenly light to see it and receive it. So here all are left without excuse.

What more could God and Christ have done for the world than they have done? What more could God and Christ, and his prophets and apostles, and his church—who are his hearers and learners—say unto you?

So if you will not hear God and Christ's speaking unto you by his son, and you have all these invitations to hear and be taught of him who is your free teacher, how can you expect anything but the judgements of God if you reject him?

Therefore this is an invitation to you all, and a warning to you all, and a testimony to you all that are called Christians, who now have time, to prize it; lest you pass away your time and it will be too late. And when time is past, you may say you had time.

So the lord God, who is the creator of all and gives life and breath to all, who takes care of all, and is over all his works, who by his son was the first and is the last speaker—direct you all; for all are to incline their ear and hear him, that their souls may live.

(Tract "To all the Kings, Princes and Governors etc.", 1676, Doctrinals pp. 603–625; Works 5/313–341)

The tenets of George Fox's teaching

After the research study had been on progress for two years, it came to mind to summarize what had been recognized of the teachings of George Fox. They were set down in very terse form, merely a series of notes. His terminology was used. They do not serve as a means of learning his teachings, but they may have value as a kind of summary or check-list.

The teachings

God is a spirit, and must be worshipped in spirit and in truth

Christ is the son of God
  God and Christ is one

Christ is spiritual, is living, is the Word

Christ, or the spirit of Christ, may be experienced directly. Is known, where two or three are gathered together in his name

The light is of Christ, is Christ

The light enlightens every one that comes into the world

The light is known in the conscience

The light reveals darkness
    shows each man his sins, evils and transgressions
    shows the good and evil in the world
    overcomes the power of the devil

The light reveals life and right living

By following or obeying the light man finds life,
    salvation and righteousness

Thus man can be saved from sin in this life;
    without pleading for sin, nor awaiting reprieve after
    death

By disobeying or ignoring the light man is left in
    darkness, spiritual death;
    and it is his condemnation

Walk in the light, be a doer, not merely a sayer

The Word was in the beginning, is now, and is eternal—
    it is outside time

The Word is the word of God

The word of God was proclaimed by the prophets,
  and by Jesus who fulfilled and completed the prophets,
  and by those who prophesy with the spirit of God

By listening in silence the word is known;
  man hears the word of God;
  it is as a command, and must be obeyed

God gives man the power to obey his word *[this is one of
  Fox's most important and emphatic teachings]*

Christ may be known in each of his offices;
  each of these offices is defined, and extensively used

As a prophet, Christ opens men to an understanding of
  (or opens man's understanding to) spiritual truths;
  and he is a teacher, a teacher from heaven, a living
  teacher

The cross of Christ is the power of God

Jesus fulfilled the prophecies of the old testament;
  he is the fulfillment of God's revelation to man;
  he is the substance of the earlier forms and shadows

Through man's love of God—which is a reflection of
  God's love of man—man comes to love other men

The spirit of the scriptures, but not the letter, is the
  spirit of God

The apostles knew the spirit of the scriptures

The scriptures are truly known with the spirit

The openings of Fox
[from his initial great mystical experiences]

He [Fox] was to bring people off the other churches

True ministry is from those who hear the word of God,
    it is not enough to have learnt at college

True ministry comes only from the pure,
    and speaks to the pure in the hearers

The other churches are in the apostacy,
    being out of the way of Jesus and the apostles,
    persecuting, and following man-made will-worship

The Lamb's war is to be waged with words,
    not with carnal weapons

The day of the coming of the Lord is nigh

He [Fox] was to establish a true church

The true church is of the believers in Christ,
    who thereby find a unity,
    who own Christ as their one authority,
    who are ordered by Christ

Men and women are to testify to the working of Christ in their lives—individually, and corporately as a church

There is that of God in every man

Men and women are equal spiritually, and in the church

God does not dwell in temples made with hands, but man is the temple of the Lord

Fox does NOT include in his teaching—

Much emphasis on the trinity

Speculation or theory on the nature of God

The divinity of Christ (in the usual sense)

Jesus' bodily resurrection

Hell or hell-fire. Original sin

Punishment for sins

The "problem of evil"

Any assertion that God is omnipotent or only-good

The authority of the written bible *[nevertheless he implies that the passages he quotes carry authority—even though he used the bible very selectively]*

By prayer, the gaining of favour, redemption, or reward, either in this life or the next

Much mention of life after death

Much mention of the incarnation of Jesus

Any significance of the virgin birth of Jesus

Any role or significance of Mary the mother of Jesus

Much emphasis on solitary worship, prayer or meditation

Fox draws DISTINCTIONS between—

Christ as a spiritual being, rather than with bodily resurrection

Baptism of the spirit, rather than outwardly by water

The Lord's Supper being spiritual, rather than in remembrance of the passover meal

True and false prophets

Ministry inspired by the spirit, rather than being of man's learning or training

Between the spirit of God and the phantastic spirit

Between prophecy and speaking in tongues

The light being of Christ, rather than natural

The light being in, but not of, the conscience

True liberty of the gospel, rather than false liberty

The Quakers' faith, rather than that of all the other churches *[those keen on ecumenical activites might note these]*

The old covenant and old testament, and the new covenant and new testament

Fox's practical witness included—

Proclamation in towns and villages. A call to repent

Ministry to church congregations and crowds

Pamphlets of doctrine and teaching

Epistles of encouragement and counsel

Comfort for prisoners and sufferers

Imprisonment of himself, to release those in inward prison

No hat worship, nor bowing to social superiors

Opposition to worldly fashions, and conventional salutations

Keep to yea and nay; no swearing

Assertion that authority of God over-rules authority of man

Silent worship is a witness of the authority of Christ

Propagation of the gospel order of the church

No other authority but Christ in the church

Guidance to Friends when they departed from the gospel order

Exhortation to magistrates and those in authority

Exhortation to parliament and rulers

Exhortation to traders etc etc against living corruptly

Further notes

These Notes were written at the end of 1977. However, they may be usefully be augmented by further comments dating from 1991 and 2008.

All the foregoing items are of the mind and intellect, they do not much touch the heart; yet Fox also touched the heart.

On reflection, there can be no doubt that Fox touched the hearts of those who met him through the charismatic quality of his personality. And this in turn was because within him there was no distinction between the indwelling divine reality and the essence of the man, the consequence of his intense mystical experience. Some of that may be seen reflected in a minority of the texts he dictated—those which were filtered out by the worthy Quakers all that time ago, but which now allow him to speak for himself.

Furthermore, it takes a great effort by us to visualize the place and effect of the concept of sin in the Church of Fox's time. The story of Adam's fall in Genesis was combined with the insidious theories of Paul about an original sinfulness we are born with, these perhaps spiced up by some of Calvin's excesses coming in from Geneva and Scotland.

All this with the concepts of torment and hell-fire were exploited by the clergy to terrify the people into a state of submission. Fox often said "they preach up sin to the grave".

Fox released 60,000 people from this tyranny. To become aware of their sense of profound gratitude requires an intensely sympathetic imagination. That gratitude was even sufficient to carry them through the persecutions that were inspired by the clergy and the magistrates.

For some (for it does not come to everyone) his presence and his example could have carried them forward to share, to a greater or lesser extent, his experience of becoming a mystic.

Section Five

George Fox on the antiquity of the Quakers

In the last years of his life, when Fox no longer had the physical energy to travel much, he wrote some documents to give guidance in the Quaker way to the 60,000 of his followers. These were included in the great volumes that Thomas Ellwood prepared around 1700, but have not been made available in modern Quaker literature.

These texts present a number of Quaker doctrines that George Fox considered important. All these themes recur again and again in his teaching, but it is unusual that they were gathered together, and each dealt with in its own right. It may be regarded as giving his view of the foundation of the Quaker faith.

Fox never claimed he was devising anything new, but only finding again the faith and teaching of Jesus and the apostles— that is what he means by using the term 'antiquity'—which had been lost during the intervening centuries. It is apparent here that Fox was primarily concerned to show how each of these doctrines was derived from scripture. To us it may come as some surprise to find the scriptural basis for much of Quaker faith.

It would also be a surprise to find that for Fox the Quaker faith has so many components. Thus while we can recognize worship, religion, beliefs, our way, our hope, our ministers and overseers, Fox added sonship of the mother, heavenly Jerusalem, timelessness of the word, the new covenant, our leader and mediator, our baptism of the spirit, and the cross that is the power of God.

The whole document is an example of Fox's fertile mind and prolific use of Biblical quotations and, it has to be admitted, is rather tedious. So only certain topics are given here, to be more relevant to our present interests. The sub-headings are Fox's own; some explanatory notes are added. The original text was first published as a pamphlet, and is included in Doctrinals pp.1012-1026 (Works 6/384-401).

Concerning the antiquity of our worship

It is that which Christ set up above 1600 years ago—when he put down the Jews' worship at the temple in Jerusalem and the Samaritans' worship at the mountain of Jacob's well—saying "The hour comes and now is, [when] they that worship the father must worship him in the spirit and in the truth."

This worship in the spirit and in the truth is above all will worshippers and dragon worshippers and the worshippers of the beast. For God has poured out of his spirit on all flesh, and grace and truth are come by Jesus.

This spirit and truth is in the hearts and inward parts of people, [so] that with the spirit of truth they may know the God of truth; and in the spirit of truth, serve and worship the God of truth. The devil, the foul spirit, and all his worshippers are out of this pure truth and holy spirit and cannot come into [it]—for there is no truth in him.

This is our pure and perfect standing worship, which Christ the son of God set up above 1600 years ago.

Now concerning the antiquity from whence we have our faith, and who is the author and finisher of it

The apostle says to the church of Christ, the hebrews "Let us run with patience the race that is set before us, looking unto Jesus the author and finisher of it."

Now here you may see the apostles did not make the saints a faith, but bid them look unto Jesus, who was the author or beginner and finisher of their holy and precious faith—the mystery of which is held in a pure conscience. So Christ reveals his faith to his people; and so they grow in faith, and from faith to faith up onto Christ, the author and finisher of it.

So this was the apostles' doctrine to the christians in primitive times, above 1600 years ago. And this is the doctrine that we have received, and own, who look at none below Jesus to be the author and finisher of our holy precious faith; in which faith all God's people please him and have access to him; which faith is our victory over that which displeases God; in which faith is our holy unity; and by this precious faith all the just live. This is the one, holy, pure, precious faith, that purifies the hearts of God's people; ... in which they have access to the holy God, and serve and please him.

So Christ is the beginner or author and finisher of our holy catholic or universal faith; in which faith the church of Christ did and [now] do build up one another, which ... Christ the holy one, and not men, is the author and finisher of.

Concerning the antiquity of our belief

Fox frequently presents the picture of when "in the beginning" man and God lived a life of obedience and harmony, only to be dashed by the first Adam; and how Jesus came as the second Adam to restore that harmony and spiritual life. And Jesus also came to fulfill or release the types and shadows of spiritual truth that had been promised in the hebraic law and spoken of by the prophets.

And as we come to see the spirit of Jesus as our rock and foundation, we are transformed into living stones, to become the living members of the fellowship of his church.

Christ, the heavenly man and second Adam, enlightens every one that comes into the world with his heavenly spiritual light, which is the life in him, the word; and by him, the word, all things were made and created.

And Christ said "Believe in the light, that you may become children of the light." So we, believing in the light, the life of Christ, are become children of the light;

and so are grafted into him, the life, in whom we have the light of life; and so are passed from the death in Adam to the life in Christ, the second Adam. And as the apostle says "He that believes, is born of God, and overcomes the world." These are the true and living members, or the living stones that make up the spiritual household, the church of Christ, of which he is the holy head.

As the apostle says "It is given us to believe" so Christ has given us the light, which is the life in himself, and says believe in the light. So we believe in that which Christ has given us, and commands and teaches us to believe in—namely, the light ... by which we may see him and know him.... This light shining in our hearts gives us the knowledge of God in the face of Christ Jesus.

This is the treasure which we have in our earthen vessels. After we believe, we are sealed with God's spirit, and can set to our seal—having the witness in ourselves—that God is true in all his promises and prophets and types and shadows in the law concerning his son Christ Jesus, ... who is our heavenly rock and foundation to build upon in this heavenly divine light. All the foundations that men lay below Christ, we cannot build upon; for as we believe in the light, the life of Christ, and are grafted into him.

And Christ says "He that believes in me has eternal life." So they that do the work of God believe in the son of God that he has sent; "he that believes shall not perish, but has everlasting life." And Christ said to

Martha "he that believes, though he were dead, yet shall he live; and he that lives and believes shall never die."

This is the true and living belief that Christ has taught us. He has given us this light to believe in—which belief is distinct from all false beliefs that men make and teach.

Concerning the antiquity of our way

Christ Jesus said "I am the way, the truth and the life; no man comes to the Father but by me."

So Christ is the new and living way, which God has consecrated for us, as in Hebrews 8:20. This new and living way Christ set up himself, above 1600 years ago, by which we come to God. And as David said "As for God, his way is perfect. It is God that girds me with strength, and makes my way perfect."

Again David says "Wherewith shall a young men cleanse his way? By taking heed of your word." So the word will keep [you] out of defiled ways.

And as Solomon says "The way or path of the just is as a shining light, which shines more and more unto the perfect day. But the way of the wicked is darkness, and they know not at what they stumble." That is the condition of those who hate the light.... You that have been astray from the light, have not you heard the word from behind you say "This is the way, walk in it"?

All you that have heard the word Christ, and so turned to him—the light, the way—you know the scripture fulfilled. The old testament was the good old way for the jews to walk in; but Christ in the new testament is the new and living way to God—to them that believe and walk in him. For God has given Christ to be a governor and leader for his people, and to be [our] salvation to the ends of the earth. So Christ—who is our leader—is our counsellor and salvation, and [our] way to God. There is no other way to the Father but by him, who has died for our sins, and is risen for our justification.

Concerning the original

John says "In the beginning was the word, etc. And all things were made by the word, and without the word was not any thing made that was made." The apostles were preachers of the word, [see] Peter 1:25. And the apostle [Paul] said "The word is nigh you, in your heart and in your mouth; and this is the word of faith which we preach." And James says "Of his own will he begat us, by the word of truth."

So God's people are begotten by the word of truth, being born again, not of corruptible seed but of incorruptible, by the word of God which lives and abides and endures for ever; and so as new born babes [they] desire the sincere milk of the word, that they may grow freely.

John says "That which was from the beginning, which we have heard, [is] the word of life; we declare that unto you, that you also might have fellowship with us. Truly our fellowship is with the Father and his son, Jesus Christ." This word is no new commandment, for John says "I write no new commandment unto you, but an old commandment which you had from the beginning. The old commandment is the word, which you have heard from the beginning." And by the word of God, which did abide in the saints, they overcame the wicked one.

"And John bore record of the word of God" and said Christ's "name was called the word of God". The word is called the word of grace, and the word of faith, and the word of power, and the word of patience; and this is the word by which all people are sanctified to them; and by this word they are reconciled to God.

This word was before the confusion of Babel, with their many languages which the priests call their original. And Pilate set a superscription in letters of hebrew, greek and latin upon Christ when they crucified him. And the beast and the whore and the false church had power over the natural tongues and languages, as in Revelation 13:7 and 17:15. But the word of God was before their tongues and languages were.

Natural men with their natural arts and sciences and tongues do not know the things of God. For natural men in their natural schools may learn their natural arts ... and religions, and so to be natural ministers.

But they that hear Christ's voice, and learn of him are bred up in his school, are made able ministers of his everlasting word.

Concerning the antiquity of our true hope, distinct from the hope of the hypocrite which perishes

"The mystery which has been hid from ages and generations is now made manifest to the saints, which is Christ in you, the hope of glory, whom we preach; warning every man, teaching every man in all wisdom, that we may present every man perfect in Christ Jesus." "And every man that has this hope in him purifies himself, even as he is pure." And we are saved by hope, as in Romans 8:24. So all the saints may know what is the hope of their calling. For we, being saved by hope, are saved by Christ who is to dwell in our hearts by faith; for the apostle said "The lord Jesus Christ who is our hope."

And we are to hold fast this hope that is set before us, which we have as an anchor of the soul, both sure and steadfast. It enters into that which is within the veil, where the forerunner is for us entered in, even Jesus. And "blessed be God, even the father of our lord Jesus Christ, who according to his abundant mercy has begotten us again unto his [living] hope, by the resurrection of Jesus Christ from the dead, to an inheritance immortal and undefiled, that does not fade away, reserved in heaven for the saints who are kept by the power of God through faith unto salvation."

Here you may see [that] the saints who are in this true and living hope have an inheritance immortal and undefiled, and are kept by the power of God, through faith unto salvation.

Concerning the antiquity of our leader, and that which gives us knowledge

The Lord said, speaking of Christ, "I will make an everlasting covenant; and behold, I will give him for a witness and a leader and a commander to the people." And "he shall feed his flock like a shepherd, and he shall gather his lambs in his arm, and carry them to his bosom, and gently lead those that are with young." "And I will bring the blind by a way that they know not, and I will lead them into paths that they have not known. I will make darkness light before them, and crooked things straight. These things I will do unto them, and not forsake them."

And Christ said he is the good shepherd that lays down his life for his sheep; and he calls his sheep by name and leads them and goes before them; his sheep follow him, for they know his voice.

Christ said he would send [to] his believers the comforter, the spirit of truth, which would proceed from the Father [and] which should guide them and lead them into all truth. So these were, and are, the ministers and teachers and disciples and believers in Christ, their leader and guide into all truth. For the apostle says that no prophecy of scripture came by the will of man, neither is it of any private interpretation; but holy men of God spake forth the scripture, as they were moved by the holy ghost. So it is the holy ghost, the comforter, the spirit of truth that leads Christ's believers into all truth, and into all the truth of the scriptures....

That which gave the church of Christ knowledge in the apostles' days gives us, the church of Christ, knowledge in our days. The apostle says "God who commanded light to shine out of darkness has shone in our hearts"—mark, in our hearts—"to give us the light of the glory of God in the face of Jesus Christ. We have this treasure in earthen vessels, that the excellency of the power may be of God and not of us." So here we have this light from God and Christ, and it shines in our hearts by God's command to give us the knowledge of his glory in the face of Christ his son. And God has the glory and honour of this light, which gives us the knowledge of Christ our saviour, who is the treasure of wisdom and knowledge....

Concerning the antiquity of the overseers

Fox uses the word "overseers" for all elders and overseers who guide the spiritual life of their people and care for them as a flock.

The apostle says unto the elders "and to all the flock, over which the holy ghost has made you overseers" etc.

Here you may see the overseers of the church of Christ were not made by men; but the holy ghost made them overseers. So they had the spiritual eye to watch over one another.

175

Christ when he sent forth his ministers told them "that they [would] be brought before magistrates and powers." And said to them "Take no thought how or what things you shall answer, or what you shall say; for the holy ghost shall teach you in the same hour what you ought to say," as in Luke 21:14–15.

So here they were to wait in the holy ghost, that led them into all truth; and not take thought [beforehand] nor follow their own thoughts, but to trust to the holy ghost, their leader and comforter.

Concerning our baptism

The following passage refers to a booklet published shortly before about baptisms and the Lord's supper—teachings now completely forgotten amongst Quakers. Relevant quotations from that have been added here between angled brackets.

The apostle says "there is one baptism". And "by one spirit are we all baptized into one body, whether we be jews or gentiles, whether we be bond or free, and have all been made to drink one spirit". So this is the one spiritual baptism, which was set up above 1600 years ago.

And you may see more of the distinction between John's baptism and Christ's in my book entitled "A distinction between the two baptisms, and the two suppers of Christ." How John's baptism, with the elements of water, did decrease; and [how] Christ's baptism, with fire and the holy ghost, increases. [Christ] thoroughly purges his floor of the heart from sin and corruption, and burns up the chaff with unquenchable fire; and how Christ gathers the wheat into his garner....

Mark—they that have been baptized into Christ are all one in him, and have put on Christ. This baptism is not into outward elementary water—for the spiritual baptism brings to put on Christ the heavenly man.... So it is clear the apostle brought people off the doctrine of many baptisms, to the one faith and one spiritual baptism. By this one spirit all were to be baptized into one body, and so all to drink into one spirit, and in that to have unity and fellowship with the Father and with his son Jesus Christ, and with one another. The Lord brings all people into this spiritual baptism and into this fellowship; amen.

This is our baptism, and baptizer.

The antiquity of our cross

The apostle says to the church of Christ "The preaching of the cross is foolishness to them that perish, but unto us that are saved it is the power of God." And such as were, and are, enemies to the cross of Christ were, and are, enemies to the power of God. So all your stone, wooden, brass, silver or gold crosses [which] you have invented and set up since the apostles' days are not the cross of Christ, the power of God, but [are] the works of your own hands.

And the apostle says "God forbid that I should glory, save in the cross of our lord Jesus Christ, by whom the world was crucified unto me, and I unto the world." So it was the power of God, the cross of Christ, the apostle glorified in.... This is our cross which we glorify in, etc, which was set up above 1600 years ago.

It is not [likely] that it was a cross made of wood, stone, iron, brass, silver or gold that the apostle or the church of God gloried in. Or that such outward, temporal and worldly crosses as men make and invent should crucify people to the world. That which crucifies people to the world, and the world to them, is the cross of Christ, the power of God; which power of God all are to bow down to, and their faith is to stand in it.

They are foolish and dark who think a cross of stone, wood, iron, silver or gold, which man has made, is the cross of Christ, the power of God. To bow to such worldly temporal things is contrary to the scriptures, which the apostles taught to the church of Christ in their days. This was the church of Christ's cross in the apostles' days, and is the church of Christ now. But they could not, nor can we, bow to any temporal, outward, worldly cross, which men have made with their hands, [nor] bow down to them. For such as worship the works of their own hands are enemies to the cross of Christ, the power of God.

Section Six

George Fox's legacy in ministry

Quakers find the best vocal ministry a high-point in their meetings for worship. It is spontaneous, unplanned, and unpremeditated. It arises from the silence like a fountain at the midst of a still pool, and the words, like drops of water, fall back again into the silence. It speaks from the heart to the heart, in a divine environment.

The first example of ministry, given on the following page, was found among the unpublished manuscripts dictated by George Fox and preserved in the Annual Catalogue. The only feasible explanation is that it was a re-creation of his ministry in a meeting for worship. (Item 15.38.F, Part 7, 1666, complete)

On page viii of the Preface I referred to a gathering which was very formative for my subsequent study of George Fox's teachings. During the meeting for worship which concluded it, when Lewis Benson rose to give ministry, the tape-recorder was switched on unobtrusively. This has given us our second example below: a precise record of ministry by a contemporary Quaker of the highest stature. Such is very rare.

179

George Fox's ministry

All you believers in the light, the power of God is your keeper unto the day of salvation. Therefore let all the believers in the light, their faith, stand in God's power—and then you will be as living plants nourished by the living God, his living springs, plants of God, growing to be trees of righteousness; and all your fruits may be unto holiness, and your end everlasting life. For God's power is his people's keeper unto the day of salvation.

In his light you will see more light till you come to the day of God; for the just man's path is a shining light, which shines more and more to the perfect day. And therefore you are commanded to believe in the light, and walk in the light, and you are kept by the power of God unto the day of salvation.

And this is the means—for the power of God is over the power of the devil, the dragon, the destroyer and the serpent, and Satan the emnity and adversary. And so the power of God your keeper is over and stronger than the power of Satan, and is able to keep you from him and all his works.

Therefore let your faith stand in the power of God which was before the devil was; for the holy divine faith which Christ is the author of must be in the power of God which is holy and divine.

Lewis Benson's ministry

The protestant mystic Jakob Böhme is sometimes rather difficult to understand, but in his little book which he called *The Way of Christ* he speaks in the simple language of the experience of faith and the experience of Christ, and tells how the word of life came to him, and how the seed—which is the word—was planted in his heart.

He comes in the end of one of his meditations to tell how he reached a place in his spiritual journey that was comparable to the growth to maturity of this little seed—of the word that had been planted in him; and how it had taken very little effort on his part.

And so he says, in the end, in a kind of wonderment, "Has my plant, while I was asleep, become a tree?"

And my prayer is that the seed, which is the word, will find a place in all our hearts to grow. And that it will grow up into a plant, and then into a tree, by the mysterious power of God that works in us whether we are asleep or awake, and keeps us and preserves us unto the day which is appointed for us.

Section Seven

A valediction

In his final years, George Fox left for Friends a document that takes the form of a valediction, a saying good-bye to his followers, the community of Quakers he had established. It comprised a message, written in his own handwriting (something that was very unusual), in a sealed envelope clearly marked not to be opened until after his death.

It is reproduced in its entirety in Ellwood's edition of Fox's Journal (pages 615–617) but has not been included in either of the modern versions, one edited by Normal Penney and the other by John Nickalls. Ellwood records that it was read to assembled Friends at their Yearly Meeting of 1691.

In it Fox recounts his ideas about his spiritual teachings, expressed in the imagery and phrases of the Bible. He uses a phrase that may be difficult for us: "New Jerusalem". This idea of a celestial city is taken from Revelations and enhanced by Paul. It stands as a symbol of a mother from whom comes sonship. This is the spiritual mother of all true christians whom she nourishes and, says Fox, find peace—elsewhere he speaks of finding love and joy there. It could well be that his hearers saw it as the community of Quakers.

No doubt these thoughts would have been reflections of the message he was giving to Meetings he visited and ministered to in his final years. He had then left his home at Swarthmoor Hall in order to be more closely in touch with the growing Quaker movement in and near London, and the seat of power and authority in Parliament and the King. He usually stayed then with one or another of his stepsons.

This was a time when some members of the Quaker community were coming up with ideas that would cause it to depart from its original form as Fox created it. An example Margaret Fell protested about was the trend for women to adopt a uniform "Quaker grey" form of dress, calling it mildly "a poor silly gospel", something we have had the good sense to get rid of. However, Fox has some stronger things to say about this. His phrase "judgement and condemnation" referred to the idea then current that opposition to the wisdom of God would lead at one's demise to a judging at the gates of heaven, with the possibility of being condemned to the torments of hell. Because the movement is structured in an extreme democratic form, with nothing like an ecclesiastical authority, it is always likely to happen. During the first decade of the twenty-first century it has happened again in Britain, with a craze for modernization, without regard for the loss of old values.

It was of course also a time of persecution by others. Fox also condemned that, but it being not now relevant, that passage is omitted. His message is here edited for modern readers in my usual manner.

To all Friends' Meetings everywhere

This is for all the children of God, who are led by his spirit, and who walk in his Light, in which they have life and unity, and fellowship with the Father and the Son, and one with another.

Keep all your Meetings in the name of the lord Jesus, that be gathered in his name by his light, grace, truth, power and spirit. By which you will feel his blessed and refreshing presence amongst you, and in you, to your comfort and God's glory.

Now all Friends, all your Meetings, both men's and women's, monthly, quarterly and yearly, were set up by the power and spirit and wisdom of God. In them you know and you have felt his power, spirit, wisdom and blessed refreshing presence among you, and in you, to his praise and glory and your comfort. So that you have been a city set on a hill, that cannot be hid....

As for this spirit of rebellion and opposition that has risen formerly and lately, and is not of the kingdom of God and heavenly Jerusalem. It is for judgement and condemnation, with all its writing, words and works. Therefore Friends are to walk in the power and spirit of God, that is over it, and in the seed that will bruise and break it to pieces. In which seed you have joy and peace with God, and power and authority to judge it. Your unity is in the power and spirit of God, and does judge it. All God's witnesses in his tabernacle go out against it, and always have and will.

Therefore all to stand steadfast in Christ Jesus, your head, in whom you are all one, male and female... and know his government, and of the increase of his government and peace there will be no end.... Therefore walk in God and Christ's light, life, spirit and power and live in love and innocency and simplicity. And dwell in righteousness and holiness....

Let no man live to self, but to the Lord, and seek the peace of the church of Christ and the peace of all men in him, for blessed are the peacemakers. Dwell in the pure and peaceable heavenly wisdom of God, that is gentle and easy to be entreated, that is full of mercy. All striving to be of one mind, heart, soul and judgement in Christ, having his mind and spirit dwelling in you, building up one another in the love of God, which edifies the body of Christ, his church, who is the holy head thereof. So glory to God through Christ in this and all other ages, who is the rock and foundation, the beginning and the ending. In him live and walk, in whom you have life eternal, in whom you will feel me, and I you.

All children of new Jerusalem, that descends from above, the holy city which the Lord and the Lamb is the light thereof. In it they are born again of the Spirit. So heavenly Jerusalem is the mother of those who receive Christ and have power given to them to become sons of God, and are born again of the Spirit. Such come to heavenly Mount Sion, and to the innumerable company of angels, and to the spirits of just men made perfect. They are come to the Church of the living God written in heaven. They have the name of God with the city of

God written on them. So here is a new mother who brings forth a heavenly and spiritual generation.

There is no schism, nor division, nor contention, nor strife in heavenly Jerusalem, nor in the body of Christ, which is made up of living stones, a spiritual house. Christ is not divided, for in him there is peace. Christ said In me you have peace. He is from above, and is not of this world. Therefore keep in Christ and walk in him. Amen.

Index of sources

The key-identifier in the left-hand column is as used in reference books. The name for each quotation is appropriate for the quotation given in this book; it may, or may not, be the same as used in other books. The right-hand column gives the page number in this book.

Manuscripts
(from Annual Catalogue unless otherwise stated)

Epistles

Original Printed Tracts

"Doctrinals"

Journal

Printed in the United Kingdom by
Lightning Source UK Ltd., Milton Keynes
139370UK00001B/32/P